THE
NEGOTIATION
CODE

**10 Proven Strategies to Redefine
Negotiation with EQ and AI**

GUY ELLIS

Editing, design, distribution by Bublish
Published by Purple Arch Publishing

ISBN: 978-1-647049-63-8 (paperback)
ISBN: 978-1-647049-64-5 (hardcover)
ISBN: 978-1-647049-59-1 (eBook)
ISBN: 978-1-647049-65-2 (audiobook)

To Alexa, my guiding star, and to my girls, my spirited negotiators—with you, every day is a lesson in love, patience, and understanding. It's for you, and with you, that I navigate life's moments. May this book stand as a testament to the beautiful balance of laughter, challenges, and love we share.

With all my heart,

Guy/Daddy

Negotiation (noun): Negotiation is the strategic craft of turning obstacles into opportunities, aligning interests with impact, and building lasting relationships through trust, insight, and intentional choices in decision-making. It's not about winning or losing; it's about unlocking potential, shaping outcomes, and creating value that transcends the deal. — Guy Ellis

CONTENTS

FOREWORD

NEGOTIATION IS OFTEN reduced to a set of tactical maneuvers—leveraging power, controlling information, and winning concessions. In *The Negotiation Code*, Guy Ellis presents a far more compelling and transformative view of negotiation. For Ellis, negotiation is not merely about securing a better deal or outmaneuvering an opponent; it is a deeply personal and strategic discipline, one that requires self-awareness, adaptability, and a commitment to continuous improvement.

This book is a call to action for negotiators at all levels. Ellis challenges us to go beyond tactics and frameworks, urging us to examine our mindset, our behaviors, and how we show up at the negotiation table. He masterfully integrates both the science and art of negotiation, combining logical strategy with emotional intelligence, structure with flexibility, and preparation with intuition. In doing so, he redefines negotiation as an exercise in relationship building, mutual problem-solving, and value creation rather than a mere contest of wills.

One of the most striking aspects of *The Negotiation Code* is its reflective nature. Unlike many books that focus solely on tactics, Ellis compels us to think deeply about the way we approach negotiations—whether in business, leadership, or daily life. He reminds us that every negotiation is an opportunity for growth, a test of character, and a chance to refine the way we engage with others. By emphasizing self-awareness and a growth-oriented mindset, Ellis makes it clear that successful negotiators are not just skilled communicators but also keen observers of themselves and others.

What makes this book particularly timely is its exploration of artificial intelligence (AI) in negotiation. In a field that has traditionally relied on human intuition and interpersonal dynamics, Ellis thoughtfully examines how AI is reshaping the negotiation landscape. His insights on leveraging AI tools—while still preserving the essential human elements of persuasion, trust, and emotional intelligence—are invaluable. In an era when data and technology increasingly influence decision-making, his perspective on AI as an enabler rather than a disrupter is both refreshing and incredibly practical.

Ellis writes not just from a place of expertise but from real-world experience. His background—spanning executive leadership, high-stakes negotiations, and personal transformation—adds depth and authenticity to his insights. He understands that negotiation is as much about managing relationships and emotions as it is about strategy and dealmaking. Throughout this book, he seamlessly bridges the worlds of professional and personal negotiation, demonstrating that the same principles apply whether one is navigating a multimillion-dollar contract or a family discussion at the dinner table.

For today's negotiator—whether an executive, entrepreneur, leader, or individual striving for better outcomes—*The Negotiation Code* is an essential guide. It offers a rare combination of strategic depth, tactical clarity, and personal reflection, equipping readers with the ability not just to negotiate better deals but to approach negotiation as a lifelong skill that can transform careers, businesses, and relationships. Guy Ellis does not just teach us how to negotiate; he challenges us to become better, more intentional, and more self-aware negotiators. And in today's complex, rapidly evolving world, that is perhaps the most valuable lesson of all.

Aram Donigian & Nolan Martin, Cofounders of NegotiateX, one of the top five podcasts on negotiation in the world.

INFLUENCE IS NOT
ABOUT PERSUADING
PEOPLE TO DO WHAT
YOU WANT. IT'S
ABOUT INSPIRING
THEM TO WANT
WHAT YOU WANT.

— *Mark McCormack*

INTRODUCTION

DRAMA. TENSION. DISTRUST. Power plays. This is what most of us think negotiations look like. In our minds, we're watching a scene out of *Succession*. No wonder the very thought of entering into a negotiation awakens our most basic human fears. Research shows significant fear associated with rejection or being seen as too pushy or too weak in a negotiation. People fear losing a negotiation and damaging their reputation or career. When business professionals enter into a negotiation, anxiety rises because they feel that there's so much at stake. This isn't surprising given our perceptions of the negotiation process. In reality, we are all negotiating throughout the day—both at home and at work—and we don't even know it. Negotiation isn't an exceptional skill reserved for the boardroom; it's a daily practice. Encouraging our kids to eat their vegetables or go to bed on time is negotiation. Navigating traffic on our way to work is negotiation. Talking to our colleagues about a strategic project or big business deal is negotiation. Peace treaties and border disputes is negotiation. Deciding where we'll take the family to dinner or go for our next vacation is negotiation. Asking for a raise or promotion is negotiation. From discussions with parents, partners, children, friends, and colleagues to high-stakes meetings with boards, investors, politicians, lawyers, employees, suppliers, partners, and clients, we are all constantly engaged in negotiations. Almost everything humans do involves some sort of negotiation. So we don't need to be afraid; we just need more confidence.

As a daily practice, negotiation is more a mindset you hone than a skill you acquire. A negotiation mindset can be improved through training and discipline. Like a muscle, it needs to be exercised daily, or it weakens. It's a use-it-or-lose-it situation. We also tend to think of negotiations as something we win or lose—but that's not the case. It's actually the opposite. Every negotiation offers an opportunity to deepen our understanding of situations and one another. Negotiations can open doors and strengthen relationships. Negotiations are not a battle of wills but a collaboration between parties seeking to achieve mutually beneficial goals. When we approach negotiations with a mindset of cooperation rather than competition, we find creative solutions that might not have been apparent otherwise. It's about exploring ways to expand the pie so everyone gets a bigger piece. This can have long-term benefits that can pay off handsomely for all parties down the road.

I wrote *The Negotiation Code* primarily for business leaders who engage in important negotiations with a variety of stakeholders every day. But this book isn't just about business deals. The practical tools I share can work in any environment, whether you're in the boardroom or at the dinner table. Learning the art of negotiation is an opportunity to create lasting, positive impacts and build meaningful connections everywhere and with everyone. *The Negotiation Code* is about transforming preconceived notions and current approaches. This book is about eliminating fear and replacing it with confidence. I'm going to break down everything into simple steps and equip you with the tools you need to approach every interaction as a healthy negotiation—one with a collaborative, growth mindset that leads to significant, sustainable, and mutually beneficial success.

With more than a decade of executive and C-suite experience, I've participated in thousands of negotiations across many industries. Through practice, discipline, and study, I've honed a unique approach that goes well beyond traditional negotiating tactics. More recently, I've incorporated artificial intelligence (AI) into my negotiating process. It has become a powerful tool that I'll teach you to harness. It's the combination of AI and human emotional intelligence, known as EQ, that makes my approach so unique.

Throughout my career, I have witnessed how effective negotiation can build bridges, solve complex problems, and create lasting relationships grounded in trust and mutual respect. These relationships, formed in the heat of negotiation, often outlast the deals themselves and become the foundation for future collaborations and successes. In one of my career-defining moments, I had the honor of facilitating a negotiation between two large rival companies with a long history of conflict. Through the steps and principles outlined in this book, my negotiating team turned a contentious situation into a collaborative partnership that revolutionized both companies' operations. The result was not just a successful deal but a transformative alliance that set a new industry standard.

Another amazing experience was when I helped a CEO transform her company's culture through the principles of skilled negotiation. By focusing on empathy, understanding, and mutual respect, she was able to renegotiate contracts, mediate internal conflicts, and build a more cohesive and motivated team. The ripple effect of her approach extended well beyond the immediate negotiations, leading to improved employee satisfaction, stronger client relationships, and a significant increase in overall business performance. These are the types of extraordinary outcomes—big and small—that I want you to experience as a result of unlocking the negotiation code.

I began my negotiation journey in South Africa, where I was born to two hardworking, middle-class parents who instilled in me the values of dedication, perseverance, and integrity. My father's entrepreneurial spirit and my mother's resilience taught me that success was not just about achieving my goals but about lifting up others, creating opportunities, and leaving a lasting impact in the world. But when I suddenly lost my father at seven years old, I had to take on responsibilities well beyond my years and navigate issues and situations atypical for such a young person. My mother was busy working and trying to hold together our altered world, so I had to self-advocate with teachers, coaches, neighbors, and friends. There was no one to guide me or negotiate on my behalf. Out of necessity, I became a confident negotiator before I could even spell the word, much less fully understand it. Navigating loss, grief, and new responsibilities at such a young age forced me to mature quickly and taught me the value of empathy, curiosity, and adaptability. I had to assess situations independently and learn from my surroundings quickly. These early lessons became the bedrock of my approach to life and work, driving me to face challenges with curiosity and compassion. I didn't realize it until I was much older, but the loss of my father at such a tender age taught me that adversity can be a powerful catalyst for growth.

But navigating life's daily negotiations without my father's guidance was often challenging. The learning curve was steep and the journey often lonely. This is the main reason I wrote *The Negotiation Code.* I want to make your road a little easier and share practical, actionable insights to help you create lasting value for all involved whenever an opportunity to negotiate presents itself—in both your professional and personal life. This book is a testament to the belief that with the right mindset, practices, and skills, we can all become skilled negotiators capable of making meaningful contributions to our companies, families, communities, and the world.

This book is a call to action, urging you to embrace the principles of negotiation not just as techniques to be learned but as a way of life that leads to growth, connection, and transformation. By fully engaging with the teachings of this book, you will be equipped to navigate any negotiation with confidence and creativity. The tools, frameworks, and insights shared within these pages are designed to be immediately applicable. By the end of this book, you won't just be equipped with negotiation tactics, you'll also understand the human dynamics that make negotiation part art and part science. You'll learn how to navigate complex situations effectively, build stronger relationships and solutions, and create lasting value in all your negotiations.

At its highest level, negotiation is a tool for transformation. Whether in business, relationships, or community, the principles outlined in this book demonstrate how negotiation can be a powerful catalyst for growth, collaboration, and change. There's no perfect way to negotiate; you have to find your own style. But by embracing the principles in this book, you will discover that negotiation is not just about achieving a favorable outcome for yourself; it's about crafting solutions that are sustainable, equitable, and mutually beneficial for everyone involved. This is what leads to something bigger, and often more valuable, than the deal on the negotiating table. The best negotiators make sure all parties feel valued and respected. This requires a shift in mindset—from viewing negotiation as a zero-sum game where one party wins and the other loses to a collaborative effort where everyone succeeds together. This shift is at the heart of *The Negotiation Code*.

I DON'T NEGOTIATE
ON TRUST,
I NEGOTIATE
ON INTERESTS.

— *Wendy Sherman*

NEGOTIATION BASICS

IN TODAY'S COMPLEX, fast-paced, and ever-changing business environment, knowing how to negotiate effectively is more crucial than ever. In the twenty-first century, many would go so far as to call negotiation a mandatory leadership skill. Think about how quickly artificial intelligence (AI) exploded on the scene, disrupting entire industries with all the challenges and opportunities inherent in those disruptions. Suddenly, everything on the internet—data, voices, written content, images, and more—is being digested by large language models (LLMs) and challenging current business models, intellectual property rights, business processes, and everyone's jobs. While some leaders have decided to stick their heads in the sand, others have started negotiating lucrative licensing agreements and partnership deals, as well as experimenting with AI inside their businesses. These early adopters have found new efficiencies and opportunities despite their limited experience in this new environment. As we will explore in-depth within this book, AI can actively assist human negotiators in every phase of negotiation. But AI is only one of many profound shifts that leaders face in today's world. The ability to navigate and negotiate in uncharted waters is quickly becoming a defining leadership trait—and one where AI can play a role.

But even as the world seems like it's spinning faster every day, the basics of negotiation have stayed much the same for thousands of years. Negotiation is as old as human interaction. Its foundations are evergreen. Why? Because at its heart, effective negotiation is about understanding people and their diverse needs, perspectives, and interests. Anthropologists and archeologists have found evidence that negotiation dates back at least two hundred thousand years, when humans bartered for basics to survive in harsh environments where food and shelter were scarce. In ancient Mesopotamia and Egypt, relics have been uncovered of early contracts and treaties written on clay tablets.

In my years of experience as a leader and negotiator across various fields and cultures, it's often the so-called "soft skills" or "people skills" that play a pivotal role in achieving successful outcomes. Planning is always key, but empathy, active listening, and authentic engagement are the foundations of any effective negotiation. By understanding and connecting with those involved and tapping into the psychological and emotional undercurrents that drive their decisions, negotiators can achieve outcomes that are not only effective but equitable, sustainable, and profoundly impactful. I am passionate about imparting these lessons to help others navigate their negotiations with confidence.

The Negotiation Code

Skilled negotiation is rooted in a holistic understanding that combines mindset and technical skills with the types of interpersonal and intrapersonal intelligences discussed by several researchers, including cognitive psychologist Dr. Howard Gardner in his Theory of Multiple Intelligences. These great thinkers posit that there are more ways to measure a person's intelligence than IQ, such as:

Emotional Intelligence (EI) or Emotional Quotient (EQ) is an intrapersonal intelligence based on a person's ability to perceive, use, understand, manage, and handle their emotions. People with high EQs use emotional information to guide their thinking and behaviors. EQ is often associated with self-awareness and self-control.

Social Intelligence (SI) or Social Quotient (SQ) is an interpersonal intelligence based on a person's ability to understand others and act wisely in human interactions and relationships. People with high SQs can effectively navigate social situations. They typically have strong listening and conversational skills.

Adaptability Intelligence or Adaptability Quotient (AQ) is an intrapersonal intelligence and is a measure of a person's ability to respond to change. It involves a set of skills and qualities that help a person adjust to uncertainty, respond effectively and quickly to new circumstances, and learn from their experiences.

Throughout my career, these intelligences have informed a multidimensional approach that has enabled me to navigate complex negotiations with a focus on long-term relationships, mutual respect, and lasting outcomes. This deep understanding of human behavior is what sets my methodology apart from traditional negotiation tactics. Whether you feel that you already possess these abilities or feel this is an area where you could use some personal and professional development, *The Negotiation Code* can help—as long as you're willing to do the work. It takes practice, but I promise it's worth the effort.

At its core, negotiation is about finding common ground, aligning interests, and crafting agreements that are not only effective in the moment but viable well into the future. This requires a deep understanding of both the art and science of negotiation. The art lies in the human touch, the intelligences we've just discussed. The science involves strategy, planning, preparation, analysis, and the use of AI. It's this unique combination that sets the stage for optimal outcomes. This is why the three pillars that underpin my approach in *The Negotiation Code* combine art and science. Here are the three pillars of skilled negotiation:

Pillar One: Employ Strategic Planning and Thinking. To achieve great things, you must define your goals, allocate sufficient time and resources, and create an effective plan or road map to achieve those goals. Human experience combined with AI research is a powerful combination in today's world. That's the strategic planning part. Strategic thinking, on the other hand, means you enter negotiations with the big picture in mind, where long-term opportunities are as important to achieve as short-term goals.

Pillar Two: Engage Multiple Intelligences. As discussed above, it's not your IQ that's going to seal the deal; it's your EQ, SQ, and AQ. The capacity to understand and manage your own emotions and biases, read the authentic mood of a room, and adapt as you go is what will position you for a successful negotiation. You should be learning about these intelligences, practicing them, and honing them on an ongoing basis.

Pillar Three: Commit to Personal and Professional Growth. I've shared my belief that life is an ongoing series of large and small negotiations inside and outside the boardroom. I'm encouraging you to shift your mindset and commit to the ongoing journey of improving your strategic planning and thinking skills, as well as your EQ, SQ, and AQ. This commitment to personal and professional growth can change the trajectory of not only your career but your entire life.

These three pillars must inform every step in the negotiating process. In *The Negotiation Code*, I define ten actionable strategies to become an effective negotiator—and each refers back to the three pillars. It's a powerful combination of ideas that I hope will help you see negotiation in a whole new light. Here are the ten strategies, almost all of which take place *before* you ever sit down at the negotiating table!

Strategy 1: Practice Your People Skills
Strategy 2: Establish Clear Goals and Objectives
Strategy 3: Plan and Prepare
Strategy 4: Harness Artificial Intelligence
Strategy 5: Craft a Unique Value Proposition
Strategy 6: Develop a Healthy, Adaptable Mindset
Strategy 7: Frame Your Position
Strategy 8: Have a Best Secondary Option (BSO™)
Strategy 9: Create Your Negotiating Grid™
Strategy 10: Bring Everything Together with the UNO™ Comparison Matrix

NEGOTIATION PYRAMID
THE 10 STRATEGIES AT A GLANCE

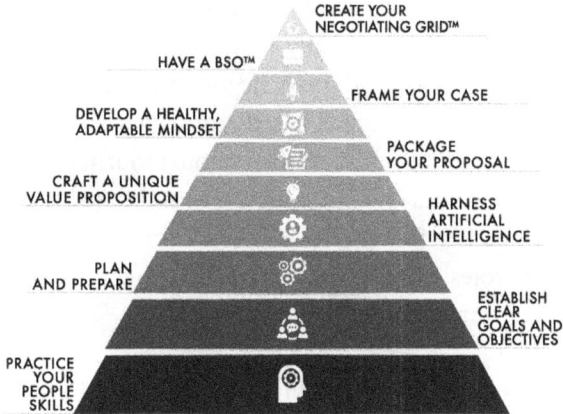

CREATE YOUR
NEGOTIATING GRID™

HAVE A BSO™

FRAME YOUR CASE

DEVELOP A HEALTHY,
ADAPTABLE MINDSET

PACKAGE
YOUR PROPOSAL

CRAFT A UNIQUE
VALUE PROPOSITION

HARNESS
ARTIFICIAL
INTELLIGENCE

PLAN
AND PREPARE

ESTABLISH
CLEAR
GOALS AND
OBJECTIVES

PRACTICE
YOUR
PEOPLE
SKILLS

Conclusion

The ten strategies—each guided by the three pillars—are foundational in any successful negotiation. Since all negotiations are simply discussions between two or more people or parties with the intention of resolving issues, creating value, or both, it's imperative to have effective planning and communication, mutual respect and understanding, and meaningful collaboration. This requires the three pillars. But I don't want to lose sight of the bigger picture here. Becoming a skilled negotiator is about understanding yourself, understanding the psychology of human interaction and negotiation, and using this wisdom to achieve great things in the world. Unlike other negotiation books that focus purely on tactics, *The Negotiation Code* is about becoming not just a better negotiator but a more confident, authentic, resilient, self-aware, and honorable leader and human at work and beyond.

Notes

_____

_____

_____

_____

_____

_____

_____

_____

_____

_____

_____

_____

_____

_____

_____

_____

_____

_____

_____

_____

_____

_____

_____

_____

_____

_____

_____

_____

_____

_____

_____

_____

_____

_____

_____

_____

_____

_____

_____

_____

_____

_____

_____

THE ART OF
NEGOTIATION IS
THE ART OF
HEARING AS MUCH
AS SPEAKING.

— *Jim Camp*

STRATEGY 1

PRACTICE YOUR PEOPLE SKILLS

SOME MIGHT ASK why I'm starting with people skills instead of planning and preparation, which is Strategy 3. It's true that practicing your people skills is part of the preparation process for any negotiation, but these skills are foundational. You should *always* be learning, practicing, and improving your people skills. Think about it like preparing for a marathon. You don't just start running a week or two before your first marathon. You might train for months or years. Running becomes part of your everyday routine. It's the same with people skills. They need to be practiced on a daily basis.

Specific negotiations may need special people skills. For example, negotiations with an international business partner might require you to research and practice new cultural norms that are important to them. I learned many important cultural lessons through negotiations. For example, in Hong Kong and China, it's important to pass things to people with both hands. If you don't, you're seen as rude. In certain African cultures, I learned, business partners won't look you in the eyes because they think that's rude. There are thousands, if not millions, of examples of cultural norms. If you're going into an international negotiation, do your homework and practice the cultural rules you need to follow to be accepted and respected by your fellow negotiators. If you don't have strong people skills, including cultural sensitivity, you're not likely to be successful in any negotiations. This is why practicing your people skills should be priority number one.

Improving your people skills means enriching your multiple intelligences. Empathy, active listening, adaptability, and authentic engagement are the foundations of strong people skills *and* effective negotiation. By focusing on the human side of negotiations, we set ourselves up to achieve outcomes that are sustainable, equitable, and profoundly impactful. Let me give you an example of what this looks like in the real world. Consider the story of a senior executive who transformed her company's approach to negotiation by shifting from a competitive to a collaborative mindset. Initially, her team focused solely on winning the deal—and they won a lot of deals. But the other parties left the negotiating table feeling shortchanged and sometimes even disrespected. Over time, some of the deals they negotiated fell apart because there wasn't a strong enough relationship between the parties to support the deal. The company's winner-take-all approach also led to strained relationships and missed opportunities for future collaboration. The writing was on the wall. The senior executive who was my client knew she had to change her negotiation strategy. Her team might have won the battle, but they were losing the war. So she decided to stop seeing negotiation as a fight and asked her team to adopt a more respectful and collaborative mindset. Over time, she was able to turn things around. They still won deals, but in a different way. They made their primary goal bigger than the deal on the table. As a result, they were able to create shared success solutions for all parties involved. This fostered goodwill and forged stronger partnerships. As a result, the executive and her team achieved more sustainable agreements and significantly enhanced their company's reputation in the industry. Ultimately, this created lucrative and expansive new business opportunities—all because they changed their strategy and decided to start putting people first. Let's dive into the specific people skills that lead to more productive negotiations.

Listen Actively

In today's distracted world, active listening is a crucial skill that is challenged by the false notion that we can multitask and absorb information from multiple inputs (text, social, email, phone calls, etc.) while still fully hearing and understanding what the person across from us is saying. Make no mistake, this is impossible. So put away your phone, make eye contact, and be fully present when you are in negotiation mode—which, as I think I've made clear, is pretty much any time you're interacting with a fellow human being. I'm being harsh because we're all guilty. However, active listening is far more than simply hearing the words spoken by the other party. It is about fully engaging with the speaker and making sure you understand their message. This involves paying attention not only to their words but to their tone, body language, and emotions. Active listening demonstrates respect and consideration, which are both critical for building trust—a cornerstone of any successful negotiation. In practice, active listening means resisting the urge to formulate a response while the other person is still speaking. It means being self-aware and understanding your own biases about the topic at hand. Active listening means remaining open-minded and focusing entirely on what the other person is saying. When you are in a state of active listening, you are acknowledging their points and asking clarifying questions when necessary. This helps you gather important information and shows the other party that you value their perspective, which often leads to more open and honest communication throughout the negotiation process.

When I was a young negotiator, I didn't fully understand the importance of active listening, and sometimes I misinterpreted what people were saying. This caused problems. Then I read about a technique called mirroring, where you listen and then make sure you've heard and interpreted their words correctly by repeating their points aloud. Most of the time, this simply led to confirmation that I'd understood. This alone, I soon realized, was a strong communication technique because it affirmed the communication and strengthened the relationship between the communicating parties. But sometimes when I mirrored something back to a person, they corrected me. These corrections were also powerful because they showed I was respectful of their ideas and wanted to get them right. I would then mirror back the correction and receive a satisfied nod. It was a simple but powerful technique that built rapport—and I've used it ever since.

Active listening means you are tuning into people's desires and values as well as looking for shared interests and experiences. You stay curious about others in all your interactions. This approach allows people to see beyond their differences and fosters deeper understanding. Whether it's a shared hobby, a similar professional background, or common life goals, focusing on these similarities can lead to deeper, more meaningful interactions. If you understand what others truly seek and acknowledge common interests and experiences, you will be in a much better position to navigate through the challenges of any negotiation. So, take time to actively listen and comprehend everyone's goals, dreams, and motivations—and discover and celebrate shared interests and experiences. This deeper level of engagement creates a powerful foundation for cooperation, innovation, and collective achievement. It offers common ground to align objectives toward shared goals and visions. It can transform relationships, turning acquaintances into loyal allies and cocreators. By striving to understand and support the aspirations of others, and recognizing your commonalities, you not only enhance your ability to negotiate effectively but to contribute to a more harmonious and synergistic environment. This paves the way for lasting, meaningful work.

Create an Empathy Map

To further enhance your understanding of the human element in negotiation, create an Empathy Map. This tool helps you systematically consider the other party's perspective. It includes four key areas:

1. What are they saying? Consider the verbal messages being communicated.
2. What are they doing? Observe their body language and actions.
3. What are they thinking? Try to infer their thoughts and concerns—to see things from their perspective.

4. What are they feeling? Assess their emotional state. Put yourself in their shoes.

By creating an Empathy Map, you gain a clearer understanding of the other party's position, informing your strategy and helping you connect on a deeper level.

Foster Mutual Respect and Trust

As the saying goes, "Don't build your house on sand." Mutual respect is the bedrock of any good relationship, and thus the foundation of any solid agreement. It's the recognition of the inherent worth of each party in the negotiation. This means you respect the people with whom you're negotiating and earn their respect in return—regardless of differences in opinion or objectives. Without mutual respect, even the most well-crafted agreements are likely to fall apart, if not during the negotiation, then soon after. This is a waste of everyone's time and resources. Mutual respect is cultivated by active listening, recognizing the other party's values, acknowledging their contributions, and treating them with fairness and dignity. When mutual respect is present, negotiations become less adversarial and more collaborative. When each party feels valued and understood, they are more willing to share information, explore creative solutions, and make concessions that lead to a shared success outcome. This is the ultimate goal of any negotiation—to reach an agreement that satisfies the needs of all parties involved. By nurturing mutual respect in your negotiations, you build relationships that are not only strong and resilient but deeply fulfilling. This can have

profound short-term and long-term benefits both profession-
ally and personally.

There's a great story that has been passed down to me
from the days of door-to-door sales. Here's how it goes: There
was a very successful door-to-door carpet-cleaner salesman
who almost got fired because he was always sitting around the
office with his feet up on the desk during the day. When his
supervisor was about to fire the salesman, he discovered the
man was actually the company's top salesman. He wondered
how this could be, so he asked the salesperson to explain
his success. Apparently, the salesperson started his day at
5:00 p.m., when all his clients arrived home from work. This
explained the salesman's lack of activity during normal business hours. But the salesman had another unusual tactic. In
the middle of his in-home pitches, he would tell his prospects
that he'd left something in his car. He'd invite his prospects to
have some fun trying out the carpet cleaner while he went to
his car, and he would leave his briefcase, filled with valuable
items like his wallet and a gold engraved pen, sitting open
somewhere in the prospect's view. When he came back in, he'd
highlight the carpet cleaner's features. He closed 90 percent
of his pitches with a sale. How? It wasn't his pitch, which was
no better than his colleagues' pitches. It was because he'd built
trust by leaving his valuables with his prospects—and trust is
central to the buying process.

If a negotiation can take place in an environment of
mutual respect and trust, both parties will refrain from fin-
ger-pointing and blaming when negotiations become challenging. If discussions become contentious, everyone takes a
breather so they can return to a state of mutual respect and
trust. This means tapping into your multiple intelligences to
"mind your mind," as they say, and take a moment to check

your biases, correct your thinking, and moderate your words and behaviors. Be mindful of your assumptions and prejudices, consciously setting them aside to maintain objectivity. This allows the conversation to flow freely, unencumbered. Mutual respect and trust are fostered by a collaborative and constructive atmosphere, which accusations can quickly erode. The blame game is a trust destroyer that makes it difficult to find common ground and reach a mutually beneficial agreement. By avoiding the temptation to assign blame, you demonstrate a commitment to understanding and resolving any issues together. This approach not only diffuses tensions but encourages open communication, empathy, and cooperation, allowing all parties to work toward a solution that addresses their needs and concerns. Remember, successful negotiation is about building bridges, not walls. By maintaining a positive and solution-oriented mindset, you create an environment in which all participants feel engaged and motivated.

One practice I believe in strongly is recognition. It encourages mutual respect and discourages negativity. If you can regularly recognize the other party's contributions and ideas throughout a negotiation, you set the tone of the negotiation. This can have a big impact on outcomes and the long-term viability of those outcomes. These do not have to be big gestures—quite the contrary. A heartfelt "thank you" or "great idea" or "good work" along with positive body language can have a big impact on the mood and overall morale in the room. It also deepens the connections between participants and can leave a lasting, positive impression on others. Genuine expressions of gratitude and acknowledgment convey respect by reinforcing the value you place on others' contributions and efforts. Over time, this approach can foster strong personal and professional bonds.

Trust is the bedrock of every meaningful negotiation. Without it, the process becomes a game of suspicion, where collaboration is replaced by defensiveness, and progress is slow, if not impossible. Building trust takes courage, consistency, and most importantly, uncomfortable transparency.

Cultivate Transparency

Uncomfortable transparency means being open—even when it's difficult. It's the practice of ensuring that nothing is left unsaid, no motives are hidden, and everyone knows exactly where they stand. It's not about oversharing or divulging every detail; it's about creating an environment in which there is no space for doubt or mistrust to grow. This kind of honesty requires vulnerability. It demands authenticity. And there is no way to fake it, no shortcut.

When done well, uncomfortable transparency creates a special bond between negotiating parties. It dismantles barriers and builds bridges, fostering a sense of safety and respect. It shows that you are not playing games or hiding agendas—that your word can be trusted, even when the truth is hard to hear. Hard conversations become the cornerstone of trust. They are uncomfortable, yes, but they are also necessary. Trust doesn't thrive on avoidance; it thrives in the light of openness, where difficult truths are confronted with courage and respect.

I remember a negotiation where uncomfortable transparency changed everything. Tensions were high, and there was an underlying suspicion that each side wasn't being fully honest. Recognizing this, I decided to address the elephant in the room. I laid everything on the table—our challenges, constraints, and even the risks we were taking in pursuing the deal. It wasn't easy (sharing vulnerabilities rarely is). But it was the turning point. The other party responded in kind, opening up about their own concerns and priorities. Suddenly, we weren't adversaries trying to outmaneuver each other. We were partners, working together to find a solution.

The bond we created through that moment of transparency didn't just make the deal possible—it made it better. Years later, that relationship continues to thrive, grounded in the trust that was built during those conversations.

Uncomfortable transparency is not without risk, but the rewards far outweigh it. It eliminates the whisper of doubt that erodes trust. It reassures people that nothing is being said or done behind their backs. It fosters authenticity in the relationship, paving the way for collaboration and mutual respect.

To build trust, you must embrace vulnerability, lean into difficult conversations, and commit to being authentic—even when it's hard. It's not easy, but it is essential. Trust, after all, isn't just a foundation—it's the bridge that turns negotiation into connection.

Be Empathetic and Kind

At its essence, empathy is the ability to understand the feelings and perspectives of others. Practicing empathy creates meaningful connection between fellow humans. In negotiation, empathy is crucial for identifying the underlying needs and concerns of others, which helps all negotiating parties craft mutually beneficial solutions. By empathizing with others, you open the door to more honest and productive discussions and more effective and enduring outcomes.

Kindness, on the other hand, is the quality of being friendly, generous, and considerate. A genuine smile, getting someone a cup of coffee or a glass of water, or simply saying, "Good morning," or asking, "How are you?" all convey warmth and openness. Authentic gestures and acts of kindness can significantly enhance the quality of interactions between negotiating parties. Do not underestimate their power. They can comfort, lift spirits, reassure, break down barriers, and diffuse tensions. Empathy and kindness pave the way for more productive and positive interactions. Setting the tone with a friendly smile encourages others to respond in kind. This simple yet powerful strategy transcends cultural and linguistic differences, making it a universal expression of goodwill. Through empathy and kindness, you create a more inclusive and supportive environment—and remind everyone that fundamental human connection is an important shared experience that unites us.

Life happens during negotiations, and sometimes people experience big, jarring life events in the middle of them. You must rise to the occasion as a fellow human being. I remember one particular occasion when the woman across the table from me lost her father unexpectedly. She was a tough negotiator, but I immediately suggested we put talks on hold for a couple of weeks so she could help with funeral arrangements. We did not know each other well, but I sent flowers with a note of condolences. I also checked in with her every few days just to let her know I was thinking of her. I'd lost my father as a child, so I could empathize. It was clear when we came back to the negotiating table that my gesture had had a profound impact on her. When we sat back down to restart our negotiations, I asked how she was, and I listened. Her pain was still very real, as would be expected, and she shared how close she had been to her father, how he'd always been her biggest cheerleader and mentor. The negotiations, which had started out rocky, went much more smoothly and resulted in a very positive outcome. We are still friends ten years later and talk to each other a couple of times a year. I hadn't sent the flowers and note to appease my negotiating partner. I'd sent them because it was the right thing to do, the human thing to do. The impact of that simple act of humanity, however, was profound. Since then, I have practiced kindness and empathy in all my negotiations. It's not a tactic; it's a commitment to being a good human above all else.

Model Effective Communication

Effective communication is the vehicle through which empathy and mutual respect are conveyed. Thus, effective communication is the gateway to trust and all its benefits. This type of communication involves not only articulating your thoughts and intentions clearly but listening actively to ensure you understand the other party's message. Effective communication minimizes misunderstandings, allows for the expression of complex ideas, and facilitates collaboration. By prioritizing clarity and openness in your communication, you create a dialogue conducive to finding common ground and reaching mutually beneficial outcomes. Trust and strong relationships are some of the benefits of effective communication, so mind your word and your body language, which is also a form of communication. Speak the truth. Learning to navigate the complexities of human relationships with grace, integrity, and confidence is an important skill for all negotiators, as it creates and nurtures connections that endure. Like mutual respect and empathy, effective communication is also a building block of trust.

Become Aware of Your Body Language

Body language plays a crucial role in the art of negotiation. While words convey explicit messages, body language reveals the underlying emotions, intentions, and reactions that may not be openly expressed. Mastering the ability to read others' body language, and control your own, can significantly enhance your effectiveness as a negotiator. When the unspoken is understood and leveraged, it can give you a distinct advantage at the negotiation table. Watch for these key body language cues:

Facial Expressions: Micro-expressions are fleeting, involuntary facial expressions that can reveal a person's true emotions before they mask them with a more controlled expression. For example, a quick frown may indicate disagreement or discomfort, even if the person is verbally agreeing with you. Steady eye contact typically suggests confidence and sincerity, while avoiding eye contact may indicate discomfort, deceit, or uncertainty. A genuine smile, of course, can ease tension, build rapport, and make you appear more approachable.

Posture and Positioning: An open posture—arms uncrossed, legs apart, and torso facing you—indicates openness and a willingness to engage. Conversely, a closed posture—crossed arms or legs—often suggests defensiveness, resistance, or discomfort. How someone sits can reflect their level of engagement—leaning in shows interest, while leaning back may signal disinterest or skepticism.

Gestures: If the other party mirrors your gestures, it's often a sign of rapport and agreement. Mirroring happens subconsciously when people feel connected or in sync with each other, and this can be effective in both face-to-face and video communications. On the other hand, repetitive movements like tapping fingers, playing with a pen, or adjusting clothes can be signs of nervousness, anxiety, or impatience.

Proxemics (Use of Space): Pay attention to how closely the other party sits or stands next to you. Invading personal space can be a sign of aggression or dominance, while maintaining a comfortable distance usually indicates respect and professionalism. In video calls, consider the space they occupy on screen—too close to the camera can feel invasive, while too far away can seem detached.

Hand Movements: Showing open palms generally signifies honesty and openness. In contrast, hiding hands or making clenched fists can suggest discomfort, tension, or even deceit. A firm handshake still remains a key indicator of confidence. On video, a firm, steady posture can convey similar levels of self-assuredness. To convey influence and authority, hold your hands in a steeple position (fingertips lightly touching while palms remain apart). This posture exudes confidence and competence, subtly signaling control and self-assuredness without appearing overbearing.

Just as you read the body language of others, they are also reading yours. Being conscious of your own body language can help you project confidence, openness, and control, which are all essential in establishing trust and authority in negotiations, whether face-to-face or online. Whether you're standing or sitting, maintain an upright posture with your shoulders back. This projects confidence and authority, making you appear more capable and trustworthy. On video calls, ensure your posture remains upright and aligned with the camera. Avoid unnecessary fidgeting, and instead, make purposeful gestures that emphasize your points. If you notice the other party's body language becoming defensive or disengaged, consider adjusting your body language to be more open and inviting. These strategies are effective in both in-person and virtual settings.

Exercise Emotional Regulation

Learning to understand your feelings and emotional triggers as well as how to self-regulate is vital if you want to be a successful negotiator. Why? Because negotiations are often exhausting and emotional. They will challenge your ability to regulate your feelings—and if you're not ready for those challenges, there's a chance you could derail discussions that might have otherwise led to something meaningful and important for you or your organization's future. You don't want to be the person responsible for this, so practice emotional regulation. What does that mean? It involves many of the other people skills discussed in this chapter like self-awareness, empathy, and active listening. But it also requires the ability to be intentional in your responses during emotionally charged moments. It means acknowledging your feelings—frustration, anxiety, anger, etc.—and learning to take command of how those feelings manifest in your body language, words, and tone. That takes a lot of discipline, so make sure you're exercising emotional regulation continuously, on a daily basis. It's the only way to prepare to successfully manage the stress of a negotiation.

Manage Your Fight-or-Flight Response

When nerves hit, your body's fight-or-flight response kicks in. This is perfectly natural but can be inconvenient and potentially unproductive in a negotiation. Here's how to understand and manage these reactions so you can stay calm and composed:

Understand Your Body's Reactions:
- **Dry Mouth and Sweaty Hands:** Nervousness causes areas like your mouth to go dry, while palms become clammy due to adrenaline.

- **Increased Heart Rate:** Your body pumps blood faster to prepare for action, which can feel like a racing pulse.
- **Temperature Changes:** You might feel hot, flushed, or even shaky.

Practice Under Pressure:

Simulate the sensation of an elevated heart rate by walking briskly or doing light exercise while rehearsing. This trains your body to perform under stress. Role-play with a trusted friend or colleague to mimic the high-pressure environment of a negotiation.

Manage Physical Symptoms in Real Time:
- **Dry Mouth:** Sip cold water to stay hydrated and refreshed.
- **Sweaty Hands:** Hold a cool object, like a chilled water bottle, to calm clammy palms.
- **Unsteady Breathing:** Focus on slow, controlled breaths. Inhale for four seconds, hold for four seconds, and exhale for four seconds.
- **Temperature Fluctuations:** Dress in breathable layers so you can adjust if you feel overheated or cold.

Ground Yourself Mentally:

- **Pause and Reset:** Take a moment to collect your thoughts. Pauses often go unnoticed but make a big difference in regaining composure.

- **Use Grounding Techniques:** Engage your senses. Identify five things you can see, four you can touch, three you can hear, two you can smell, and one you can taste. This keeps you present and focused.
- **Visualize Success:** Picture yourself walking into the room confidently, articulating your points clearly, and achieving your desired outcome. Visualization helps your brain rehearse success.
- **Smile and Stand Tall:** Smiling and maintaining good posture can trick your brain into feeling more confident while also projecting assurance to others.

Hold Yourself Accountable

Being responsible for your actions and decisions is fundamental to building and maintaining trust in any relationship, whether personal or professional. By owning up to your choices and their outcomes, you demonstrate integrity and a commitment to transparency. This willingness to accept responsibility, especially in challenging or unfavorable situations, shows others that you are reliable and trustworthy. It reassures everyone involved in the negotiation that you are not only capable of making decisions but prepared to stand by them and address any issues that may arise. This encourages open communication and fosters an environment in which people feel safe and respected. This gives people confidence that you can pave the way for deeper, more meaningful connections and collaborations. Ultimately, embracing accountability in all aspects of your life enhances your credibility and inspires others to do the same, creating a culture of trust, respect, and mutual support.

The flip side of accountability is owning your limitations. No one is perfect. We all have shortcomings. This is the essence of self-awareness. Recognizing your weaknesses during a negotiation can foster authentic connection and create an environment in which others feel free to let down their guard and be humble and empathetic. But it takes courage. When we acknowledge our imperfections and areas for improvement, we open the door to genuine, transparent communication. The door is open for a negotiation that becomes a journey of growth and learning. Others feel able to share their vulnerabilities, leading to more authentic and meaningful interactions. This approach also helps everyone move past judgment and blaming and choose instead a mindset of support and collaboration. It can break down barriers and build bridges, leading to a sense of solidarity and mutual respect. Humility and compassion foster an environment in which effective teamwork thrives, relationships strengthen, and collective success becomes achievable.

Motivate and Celebrate

Nobody wants to be told, "Just do it." When tasks are framed as purposeful and beneficial, people understand why they need to do the job well. They are pulled rather than pushed to complete each task. Make time to highlight the benefits of each task throughout the process—and do this proactively. Consider starting each day on a positive note with a motivational reminder of what everyone is trying to achieve and why it's important. Everyone should know the core values, core purpose, and core vision. As in business, this is also so important in negotiations. Paint a vivid picture of the potential rewards and growth. Emphasize how these tasks can lead to personal and professional development, increased satisfaction, or improved efficiency. Use authentically encouraging language that inspires confidence and enthusiasm. Help those who are struggling to see their contributions as important. By demonstrating your support and offering guidance, you can alleviate concerns and foster a positive, purposeful, and productive environment.

When modifications are proposed in a negotiation—which is almost always the case—lay the groundwork for open dialogue to work through potential frustrations. This is when motivation really matters. It might take a slightly different tone, but there's an opportunity to articulate how the modification can enhance the other party's experience, improve outcomes, or address specific challenges. Highlight the benefits in a manner that reflects collective values and priorities. Making it clear that the well-being of all is at the heart of the proposed changes is a form of motivation. Use positive, inclusive language that fosters a sense of partnership and shared goals. Emphasize that these modifications are designed to create a more favorable and supportive *environment*, ultimately contributing to the other party's success and satisfaction. This approach not only makes the proposed changes more acceptable but strengthens the relationships of all parties, paving the way for future collaboration. Ultimately, by motivating everyone through the modifications, you create a more harmonious and productive environment that reinforces everyone's commitment to shared success despite any obstacles.

And don't forget to celebrate! In a negotiation, especially long ones, every step forward is worth celebrating because it signifies progress. Recognizing and honoring even small victories motivates continued effort and dedication. Each incremental advance, no matter how modest, represents a triumph over challenges and obstacles. Celebrations are a testament to perseverance and resilience and encourage everyone to appreciate the journey, not just the destination. They remind the entire negotiating team that success is built through a series of small, consistent efforts. Even a small celebration can shift everyone's mood. It can encourage and foster hope. This reinforces the belief that progress is possible and every effort counts. In turn, this positive reinforcement boosts morale and strengthens everyone's resolve. In both personal and professional contexts, taking the time to celebrate small achievements can create a ripple effect. It can motivate and inspire, especially on the tough days. This could be in the form of a lunch, dinner, or even drinks at the office.

BEACONS: A Framework for Influence

Strong people skills and emotional intelligence are the cornerstone of successful negotiations and leadership. One particularly effective tool for enhancing your influence and communication is the BEACONS framework. Originally developed to help professionals manage upward within organizations, it is equally powerful in a wide range of scenarios, from navigating complex personal relationships to influencing high-stakes negotiations. The BEACONS framework is built around seven key principles, each designed to help you foster trust, engage with others effectively, and overcome obstacles:

B – Build Influential Alliances

Focus on creating authentic connections with open-minded individuals who share or support your vision. Engage stakeholders in meaningful conversations and foster collaboration to achieve a shared goal. For example, before presenting a new idea in a negotiation, take the time to understand key stakeholders' perspectives and garner their informal support.

E – Engage with Empathy and Patience

Emotional intelligence requires seeing the world through others' eyes. Recognize the pressures others face and approach interactions with empathy. Patience demonstrates that you value their perspective and builds trust over time.

A – Adapt

In negotiations, sticking rigidly to one idea can alienate others. Instead, be adaptable and focus on the broader goal, thereby showing your willingness to collaborate. This flexibility opens the door to creative solutions that may not have been apparent initially.

C – Communicate with Clarity

People respond well to clear, logical arguments supported by evidence. Prepare thoroughly, whether it's data, case studies, or persuasive anecdotes. Present your case with confidence but allow room for discussion.

O – Optimize Timing

Timing can make or break your efforts to influence others. Know when the decision-makers are most receptive and choose moments when your proposal aligns with their priorities. This could mean waiting for a scheduled review meeting or presenting your ideas during a time of opportunity.

N – Navigate Feedback

Be open to constructive criticism. Feedback is not a roadblock; it's a tool for refinement. By listening and showing a willingness to incorporate others' ideas, you foster a sense of collaboration and mutual respect.

S – Stay Resilient

Resilience and persistence go hand in hand as the foundation of successful negotiation. Setbacks and challenges are inevitable, but persistence ensures you remain focused and determined, even in the face of obstacles. Treat every hurdle as an opportunity to learn, adapt, and refine your approach. By staying committed to your goal and pressing forward with resolve, you not only build trust but demonstrate the strength and dedication needed to achieve meaningful outcomes.

BEACONS Beyond the Workplace

Although the BEACONS framework was originally designed to enhance workplace influence, its principles are universal. Whether you're navigating a family decision, leading a community initiative, or mentoring someone, BEACONS can illuminate the path forward.

For example, imagine trying to convince a family member to pursue a healthier lifestyle. Building alliances (B) might involve enlisting the support of other family members, while engaging with empathy (E) helps you address their concerns without judgment. Adapting flexibly (A) by suggesting small, manageable changes shows you're invested in their well-being. Each principle works seamlessly to create a foundation for mutual understanding and shared progress.

The BEACONS framework is a practical way to practice emotional intelligence in real time. By combining empathy, adaptability, preparation, and resilience, you can influence others effectively while maintaining a spirit of collaboration and trust. Integrating BEACONS into your negotiation and relationship-building strategies will not only enhance your outcomes but also strengthen your connections in every area of life.

BEACONS™ FRAMEWORK

- **B**UILD INFLUENTIAL ALLIANCES
- **E**NGAGE WITH EMPATHY AND PATIENCE
- **A**DAPT
- **C**OMMUNICATE WITH CLARITY
- **O**PTIMIZE TIMING
- **N**AVIGATE FEEDBACK
- **S**TAY RESILIENT

How to Build Your EQ, SQ, and AQ

Take a few moments to reflect on a few of your recent negotiations. Ask yourself:

- How did this negotiation make me feel (before, during, and after)?
- How did I manage my emotions during the negotiation? Were there moments when negative or positive emotions influenced my decisions or behaviors? When this happened, how did it impact the other people in the negotiation and the outcomes?
- Was I transparent? Did I do enough to allow others to feel they could be transparent, and were they? How did I overcome the discomfort, and was I vulnerable?
- Did I actively listen to all participants in the negotiation? Was I engaged, kind, and empathetic throughout, or did I struggle in any of these areas? Did I table my own biases in order to listen with an open mind, or did I interrupt or make decisions before people finished sharing their ideas?
- Did I seek out commonalities and shared experiences with others? How well did I understand everyone else's feelings and perspectives?
- Did I pick up on any signs of frustration, enthusiasm, or hesitation? If so, how did I handle this awareness?
- What did I do well in this negotiation? What could I do differently in future negotiations to enhance my own emotional intelligence to the benefit of myself and others?

- Have I sought feedback from others to improve my self-awareness, EQ, SQ, and AQ?

Write down your reflections and consider how you can apply these insights in your next negotiation.

Conclusion

There is a unique satisfaction that comes from achieving a mutually beneficial agreement. Knowing you've contributed to a winning outcome that is fair, just, and sustainable for all involved is very rewarding. It allows you to experience the full potential of effective negotiation and demonstrates that your work on your people skills has paid off. You've transformed your approach to communication, decision-making, and relationship building and embraced a mindset that values empathy, collaboration, and integrity. By doing so, every negotiation has become an opportunity for personal growth and creating lasting, positive relationships and impacts.

Notes

_____

_____

_____

_____

_____

_____

_____

_____

_____

_____

_____

_____

_____

_____

_____

_____

_____

_____

_____

_____

_____

_____

_____

_____

_____

_____

_____

_____

_____

_____

_____

_____

_____

_____

_____

_____

_____

_____

_____

_____

_____

_____

_____

_____

_____

_____

IN BUSINESS,
YOU DON'T GET
WHAT YOU DESERVE,
YOU GET WHAT
YOU NEGOTIATE.

— *Chester L. Karrass*

STRATEGY 2

ESTABLISH CLEAR GOALS AND OBJECTIVES

IT'S ESSENTIAL TO enter every negotiation with a clear and precise understanding of what you aim to achieve and how you're going to get there. So establishing clear goals and objectives from the start is central to negotiation. Goals are the outcomes you wish to achieve, while objectives are the measurable, short-term actions you will take to achieve those goals. This clarity of purpose combined with a road map will not only guide your approach but will provide a solid framework to stay focused and aligned with your desired outcomes. Of course, it is equally important to stay flexible and recognize the important role of concession in negotiation. In fact, defining these areas might be an objective to achieving your bigger, long-term goals. So make sure to consider this as part of the objective-and-goal-setting process. Adaptability allows you to navigate unforeseen challenges, accommodate new information, and adjust your approach to better meet the evolving needs of all parties involved. By balancing goals, steadfastness, and adaptability, you're setting yourself up for a productive negotiation process. You know what you want to achieve but remain open to the most innovative and promising solutions. Embracing this mindset not only increases your chances of success but also fosters a more positive and cooperative negotiation environment in which mutual respect and understanding can flourish. Ultimately, this balanced perspective empowers you to achieve your goals while building stronger, more enduring relationships with your negotiation counterparts. This can lead to surprising benefits down the road.

Define Clear Goals

To be effective as a negotiator, you must follow the SMART framework, which means goals must be specific, measurable, achievable, relevant, and time-bound. Most companies, and individuals, have multiple goals, so it's important to establish a hierarchy. Prioritize what matters most and identify areas where concession is possible. There are often areas of non-negotiability, so make sure they are clearly defined alongside areas where flexibility can be exercised. Understanding your goal hierarchy can help you maintain focus and ensure you achieve that which is truly important to you. By knowing what matters most, you can defend your critical objectives with conviction while having the necessary bandwidth to make concessions that do not undermine your primary goals. Your goals must be ambitious and strategically aligned with the strengths and weaknesses of the other party's Best Secondary Option (BSO™), which we will explore in-depth in Strategy 9. It's important to distinguish between these two concepts: your goal should be informed by their BSO, while your reserve is determined by your own BSO.

Primary Goals

Like all goals, effective primary goals should follow the SMART framework and be closely aligned with your broader strategic goals—whether personal, professional, or both. A well-defined primary goal not only gives you a clear target but helps you effectively communicate your desires to others. If you're negotiating a business deal, your primary goal might be to secure a partnership that generates $1 million in revenue over the next year. In a personal scenario, such as discussing shared responsibilities with a partner, the primary goal could be to establish over the next week an equitable division of chores that balances each person's workload. How you go about achieving either of these goals is mapped out with objectives.

Secondary Goals

While your primary goal is at the top of the hierarchy, secondary goals are additional outcomes you'd like to achieve. These might include securing a longer contract term or gaining additional resources or market data. Secondary objectives can serve as valuable bargaining chips during a negotiation. In a personal context, such as planning a family vacation, secondary goals might include ensuring the trip is both educational and relaxing or finding activities that cater to different age groups. Create a prioritized list of secondary goals. Consider ranking them by importance and by flexibility, so you know which ones are open to compromise and which ones are not.

Ultimate Goals

Beyond the primary and secondary goals of a negotiation, it's important to consider ultimate goals. These are typically longer-term goals—and more strategic. For example, after a preliminary negotiation, you might seek to establish a long-term relationship or partnership with the other party whereby they become an advocate for you. If this is the ultimate goal, it would certainly impact all negotiations. So, before every negotiation, write out your ultimate goals and make sure you understand where they belong in your goal hierarchy. Working through this exercise is sure to enrich your thinking and your preparation for your negotiation.

Examples of Goals

To help you understand what different types and levels of goals look like in the real world, here are some scenarios to explore and ponder.

Essential Needs: Aim to directly address the most pressing needs of the other party, ensuring your solutions are tailored to meet their specific challenges and objectives. In a personal context, this could translate to addressing the emotional and practical needs of family members during a negotiation, such as ensuring that everyone's voice is heard and that solutions are practical and considerate of all involved. Imagine you're negotiating a healthcare technology contract with a potential client whose primary objective is to enhance patient engagement. For a personal scenario, consider a family discussion about health and wellness goals, where the objective might be to agree on a collective plan for improving family fitness levels. Both scenarios require understanding the core needs and aligning your approach to address them effectively.

Relationship Building: Specify whom you need to build relationships with and establish a clear timeframe for doing so to ensure strategic and impactful networking. This principle applies in personal life as well, where building strong relationships with key people—such as mentors, friends, and family members—requires a clear and intentional approach. Imagine you've identified that building a relationship with the chief medical officer (CMO) of a prominent hospital network would significantly benefit your organization. Understanding their personal needs, interests, and challenges allows you to connect more meaningfully and build a foundation for long-term business collaboration. In a personal context, you might focus on building a stronger relationship with a mentor or family member, which also requires the same kind of understanding.

Unique Value Proposition: Differentiate yourself, your company, product, or service to make a lasting impression by showcasing the unique value and distinctive qualities that set you apart from the competition. In personal negotiations, highlight your unique strengths—such as patience, empathy, or problem-solving skills—to positively influence the outcome. During a negotiation for software services, for example, strategically high-lighting your product's unparalleled security features can serve as a powerful differentiator, setting your business apart from the competition. In a personal context, consider how your unique qualities—such as your knack for organization or your ability to be a calming presence during stressful times—can be highlighted to strengthen your position in a community project. This is strategic messaging—a compelling way to communicate what you do without focusing solely on the literal function.

Extended Engagement: Look to grow your influence with customers or within personal relationships over time by fostering trust, value, and continuous engagement. This could involve maintaining ongoing communication, showing appreciation, being transparent and vulnerable, and continually finding ways to add value to the relationship. Suppose your company offers a comprehensive suite of services designed to meet various client needs. In this case, you must ensure that each interaction reinforces trust and highlights your commitment to solving their problems. This means actively listening to their evolving needs, anticipating challenges they may face, and tailoring your solutions to provide consistent and meaningful value over time. In personal life, this might involve continuously supporting a friend or family member through consistent communication and assistance, thus deepening the relationship and ensuring mutual reliance over time.

Peer Recommendations: Seek to gain referrals as a marker of a successful negotiation by consistently delivering exceptional value and fostering strong, positive relationships throughout the process. In life, this could mean earning the respect and trust of others, who then speak positively about you within your community or network. Consider incorporating a strategic clause in your negotiation that stipulates the client's agreement to provide a written testimonial or serve as a reference for future potential clients. In a personal context, this could mean mentioning that you have experience with an issue a friend is dealing with and offering to set aside some time to chat about it, which can lead to further opportunities for collaboration or support.

Customer Reliance: Strategize ways to increase a customer's dependency on your services by consistently delivering exceptional value, innovation, and support. One strategic objective could be to bundle your offerings in a comprehensive package that provides significant advantages for the client, encouraging them to source multiple services from your company rather than from various providers. It could also be opening doors for them that cost you nothing but have a huge impact on them. This is one of the easiest and most powerful techniques I use to create immense goodwill and foster a sense of mutual support. When done with genuine kindness and authenticity, this approach is so powerful that it has the potential to transform the way you negotiate entirely. In personal relationships, this might involve being the go-to person for advice or support because of your reliability and expertise. And in personal negotiations, consider bundling commitments, such as combining a family vacation with educational opportunities for children, making the proposition more attractive to everyone involved.

Expert Showcase: Use the negotiation as a platform to showcase your expertise by strategically highlighting your skills, knowledge, and accomplishments. This can apply in personal situations as well, where you might demonstrate your competence in areas like financial planning, home management, or conflict resolution to build trust and influence. If you are negotiating a consulting contract with a healthcare or medical entity, set an objective to include a pilot project that offers your team the opportunity to showcase their expertise in streamlining healthcare operations. Creating a unique, trademarked assessment is an excellent way to open doors and establish a strong initial connection for yourself or your organization. In a personal context, you might demonstrate your expertise in organizing events by successfully planning a family reunion, showcasing your skills in coordination, budgeting, and communication.

Profit Maximization: In every negotiation, a critical objective should be crafting agreements that not only create a shared success outcome for both parties but also optimize your margins to protect and enhance the financial health and sustainability of your business. This doesn't mean focusing solely on short-term gains; instead, it involves thinking strategically about the broader picture. Consider how the terms you negotiate will impact future opportunities, ongoing relationships, and the ability to scale or adapt. A well-negotiated agreement should not only meet immediate needs but also position you for long-term success. In personal negotiations, the principle remains the same: strive for fairness while ensuring the decisions you make align with your long-term goals and well-being. It's important to recognize that while compromises may sometimes be necessary, they should not come at the expense of your overarching priorities or values. For example, in a negotiation with a close friend or family member, being overly generous might feel right in the moment but could create unintended consequences later.

Profit maximization isn't just about numbers; it's about building a foundation that supports sustained growth and enduring relationships. By focusing on creating value for both parties while ensuring your interests are protected, you set the stage for outcomes that are not only beneficial but mutually rewarding in the long run. In doing so, you reinforce the importance of strategic thinking and balance in every negotiation, whether in business or personal contexts.

Conclusion

Entering a negotiation without clear objectives is akin to sailing a ship without a compass. While you may make a little progress, you will ultimately be rudderless and fail to reach your destination. Just as a compass provides essential guidance and orientation for a mariner, your well-defined goals will steer you through the negotiation process. Setting clear goals from the outset ensures you arrive at your desired outcome. As long as your goals are specific, measurable, attainable, relevant, and time-bound, you'll have an effective framework to navigate even the stormier parts of your negotiation. With a clear sense of direction, you can make informed decisions, prioritize effectively, and stay focused on what truly matters. Your goals will serve as a constant reference point, but you'll be able to adapt to changing tides because you've prioritized them and strategically defined areas of potential concession. This allows you to navigate any negotiation with confidence and precision.

Notes

_____

_____

_____

_____

_____

_____

_____

_____

_____

_____

_____

_____

_____

_____

_____

_____

_____

_____

_____

_____

_____

_____

_____

_____

_____

_____

_____

_____

_____

_____

_____

_____

_____

_____

_____

_____

_____

_____

_____

_____

_____

_____

_____

_____

A NEGOTIATOR
SHOULD OBSERVE
EVERYTHING. YOU
MUST BE PART
SHERLOCK HOLMES,
PART SIGMUND FREUD.

— *Victor Kiam*

STRATEGY 3

PLAN AND PREPARE

JUST TO BE sure we're all on the same page, planning and preparation are not the same. Planning is about plotting a course and identifying steps to achieve a goal, which is important in any negotiation. Preparation involves actively undertaking those steps.

It's a good first step because it's about predicting the future and creating a road map to move through that future efficiently. However, it's imperative to equip yourself with comprehensive data and insights before any negotiation. Knowledge is indeed power, which means thorough research is the best generator. That is preparation. Part of this is about knowing your audience. I'll give you an example from earlier in my career when I used to try to impress my negotiation partners with the fact that I'd been involved with private equity funds, but I never got the desired effect. Instead of being impressed, my negotiating partners' faces dropped. It took me a while to realize that many people, all around the world, blamed hedge funds and Wall Street in general for the financial crisis of 2008. A lot of doors closed in my face back then because I didn't understand this. If I'd have done thorough research, I would have understood this. I wouldn't make this mistake going forward.

By delving deeply into relevant information about the market, the other party's needs and constraints, historical data, and potential outcomes, you prepare yourself to anticipate objections, identify opportunities for mutual gain, and craft proposals that are both compelling and realistic. But as any business leader knows, things rarely go according to plan. That's where preparation comes in. Preparation is about learning, practice, and gaining experience. It's about developing the skills and types of intelligence you need to react quickly and effectively in the moment. If you're practicing the three pillars, you're preparing for your next negotiation, even if it's not on the books yet. Meticulous planning and preparation transform your negotiation strategy from a mere idea into a robust framework capable of achieving successful and sustainable outcomes. This approach ensures you can negotiate with the confidence and insight needed to turn challenges into opportunities, achieving the best possible result. If I may suggest one thing you can start today, it's practicing uncomfortable transparency. This paves the way for clear communication, and when done well, it is transformational. In planning, it's transformative because it eliminates the need for constant guessing or exhaustive research, saving time and energy while providing invaluable clarity and focus.

Planning Basics

Let's start with the planning basics. As I mentioned, this is about predicting how a negotiation might go and plotting a course to navigate through that prediction. Here are my top planning basics:

Confirm Willing Partners: Always remember that for a negotiation to take place, *both* parties must be willing and able to engage in the process. This mutual readiness is the foundation upon which successful negotiations are built. Before diving into the details, take a moment to ask yourself, "Is this person (or organization) ready to enter into a productive negotiation with me?" This critical question prompts you to assess the situation carefully, ensuring both you and the other party have a genuine interest in reaching an agreement and possess the necessary authority and resources to do so. Recognizing the willingness and capability of both sides to negotiate creates a level playing field, paving the way for open, honest, and productive dialogue and problem-solving. You want to understand the answer to this question—and all the other questions it raises—before moving forward. Because if both partners aren't willing, negotiation is impossible—and nothing more than a waste of your precious time and resources. If the other party isn't immediately willing, it doesn't mean the door is closed; it means it's time to focus on strengthening your people skills and building a genuine relationship with them. I often say the best negotiation occurs when the other party doesn't even realize they're in a negotiation. This isn't about manipulation or hidden agendas; it's about authentically adding value to their life with kindness, empathy, transparency, and vulnerability. By doing so, you create opportunities for future discussions, founded on a strong bedrock of trust and mutual understanding. When that moment comes, the negotiation will feel natural and collaborative, built on the foundation of the relationship you've cultivated.

Define Purpose, Objectives, and Goals: Purpose-driven negotiation is at the heart of effective strategy. Your objectives are not just targets to hit; they embody your company's long-term vision. When you enter a negotiation with a clear purpose, you bring a sense of direction that guides every decision and interaction. This is true in both business and life. Whether negotiating a business deal or setting household rules, having a clear purpose ensures all parties understand the bigger picture. We're going to dive into this multifaceted topic much more deeply in the next strategy, but it's worth mentioning here because it is central to the planning and preparation process.

Clarify Core Values: Before entering any negotiation, take time to reflect on your core values. Ask yourself how the objectives you're setting will contribute to your long-term vision. This reflection will guide your strategy and help you make decisions that are both effective and meaningful. You see, negotiation is not about winning but about achieving outcomes that align with your core values and long-term goals. Whether in business or personal life, it's crucial that your objectives reflect what truly matters to you. This alignment ensures your negotiations are not just transactions but steps toward a greater purpose.

For example, if one of your core values is having fun, your objectives might include creating a positive and enjoyable atmosphere during the negotiation, which can lead to better rapport and more collaborative outcomes. While integrity and honesty are table stakes—nonnegotiable and essential for any interaction—an element of fun can transform the dynamic.

For instance, I once entered a high-stakes negotiation where the tension was palpable. To break the ice, I made a lighthearted joke about the overly complicated coffee order I'd just placed. The room laughed, and it instantly changed the tone of the discussion. That moment of shared humor helped everyone relax, paving the way for a more open and constructive conversation. Injecting a bit of fun reminded all of us that while the stakes were high, we were still people, working together to find common ground.

Fun in negotiations isn't about being unprofessional; it's about creating an environment in which people feel comfortable, engaged, and connected. When done right, it can enhance trust, creativity, and cooperation, making it a powerful tool for success. In a personal negotiation, such as setting curfews with your teenage children, your core value of having fun might lead you to prioritize an agreement that balances your objectives of freedom with accountability. Aligning your objectives with your values ensures you walk away from the negotiation not just with a win but with your principles intact.

Set Success Metrics: Once you know clearly what you want to achieve, you can define how you will measure the success of your negotiation. It's a crucial step that sets clear benchmarks for evaluating the outcomes. Success can be multifaceted, encompassing various dimensions such as achieving your primary objectives, fostering positive relationships, and ensuring long-term benefits.

Start by being specific about your goals: Are you aiming for a particular financial gain, securing a strategic partnership, or achieving a mutually beneficial agreement? In a personal context, success might be measured by the level of satisfaction and harmony achieved within a family decision-making process.

Assess Concessions: Think of concessions like a negotiation currency. They are the elements you're willing to give up or compromise on, and they play a crucial role in shaping the dynamics of your negotiation. Concessions can be valuable assets you can leverage to create a balanced and mutually beneficial agreement. Understanding and identifying these negotiable points beforehand empowers you to enter discussions with a clear strategy, ready to make thoughtful concessions that do not undermine your core objectives. Follow these three simple steps to prepare:

1. *List Each of Your Concessions:* List all potential concessions, including pricing flexibility, service add-ons, delivery timelines, making valuable introductions for the other party, etc.
2. *Rank Concessions by Importance:* Rank these concessions in order of their importance. What can you afford to give up, and when? What is nonnegotiable?
3. *Develop a Strategy for Each Trade Point:* Determine how you'll introduce each trade point during the negotiation. Will you present it early as a goodwill gesture, or will you hold it back as a last-resort concession?

The true power of a well-negotiated deal doesn't lie in the concessions you make but in how meticulously you have prepared to turn those investments into strategic advantages. (By the way, did you notice how I framed concessions as an investment in the deal instead of a sacrifice?) By identifying what you are willing to give up—or rather, invest in the deal—you can enter negotiations with a clear strategy that allows for flexibility without compromising your core objectives. Equip yourself with comprehensive data and insights about the other party, market conditions, and comparable deals to strengthen your position and anticipate potential challenges.

Create a Research Folder: The knowledge and insights you gather before a negotiation become your ammunition and fortify your negotiating stance. The more you know about the other party's needs, motivations, and constraints, as well as the prevailing market conditions and comparable deals, the stronger and more resilient your position becomes. Leverage all available public records, reports, and statistical data to reinforce your arguments during the negotiation. By grounding your points in concrete, reliable information, you bolster your credibility and present a compelling, fact-based case. This comprehensive understanding equips you with the ability to anticipate their moves, proactively address their concerns, and propose solutions that resonate deeply with their interests. I suggest you create a research folder to arm yourself by compiling all relevant research into one document with the following key aspects.

- *Market Analysis:* Current trends, key players, and economic factors affecting your industry.
- *Competitor Benchmarks:* How similar deals have been structured and what terms were agreed upon.
- *Client Profile:* A detailed overview of the other party's business, including financials, market position, and strategic goals.
- *Data Sources:* List reliable sources for industry data, such as market reports, financial statements, and public records.
- *Key Statistics:* Identify key statistics that support your position (e.g., market share, revenue growth, cost benchmarks).
- *Geographical Synergies:* Demonstrate how your products or services align with the client's regional objectives.
- *Client Satisfaction Stats*: Strengthen your negotiation position by showcasing compelling data on client satisfaction and retention.
- *Potential Urgent Business Needs*: List what you believe the other party's most pressing business and personal needs are currently.

Consult Multiple Teams: If you're part of a larger organization, try engaging multiple departments in your research to gain a comprehensive understanding and robust perspective. By incorporating input from diverse departments, you benefit from a wide range of expertise and viewpoints, leading to a more informed and strategic negotiation. Make sure to include top experts from each department to get the best minds involved.

Consider holding a cross-departmental strategy meeting, during which you can review the following:

- *Agenda:* Prepare an agenda that includes key points of discussion for each department (finance, sales, legal, etc.).
- *Key Insights:* After the meeting, compile the key insights from each department into a cohesive negotiation strategy.
- *Follow-Up:* Schedule follow-up meetings to reassess your strategy as the negotiation progresses.
- *Research Folder:* Add your cross-departmental findings to your folder.

Study Comparables: Thoroughly study similar negotiations or deals to gain valuable insights and lessons that can inform your strategy. By examining past negotiations, you can understand the dynamics, challenges, and strategies that led to their outcomes. I recommend a case study comparison:

- *Case Study 1:* Detail a past negotiation that went well. What were the key factors? What lessons can be applied to your current situation?
- *Case Study 2:* Analyze a negotiation that didn't meet expectations. Identify the pitfalls and consider how they could be avoided.
- *Action Plan:* Based on these case studies, outline your strategy for the current negotiation. Include contingencies for potential challenges. Add this all to your research dossier.

Analyze the Other Party's Needs: Beyond comparable deals, it's crucial to fully understand the other party's specific needs and challenges. Uncover what drives them, what their core objectives are, and where their pain points lie. By gaining a comprehensive understanding of their needs and concerns, you can tailor your approach to align with their priorities and demonstrate how your offering is uniquely positioned to provide value. I suggest creating a Needs Analysis Worksheet with the following items:

- *Key Drivers:* Identify the other party's key drivers (e.g., cost savings, market expansion, operational efficiency).
- *Pain Points:* What challenges are they facing? How can your offer address these issues?
- *Alignment Strategy:* Develop a strategy that aligns your strengths with their needs.

Preparations Basics

Preparation, as I mentioned, is about training, practice, and gaining experience so you can react quickly and effectively in key moments during negotiations. It's learning about your strengths and weaknesses as a negotiator and knowing your company and your people inside and out. You should always be preparing for your next negotiation, and you should always be assessing your performance in the last one. Preparation is about constant improvement. Practicing your people skills and the three pillars have already been covered, so I won't repeat them here. But make no mistake, they are by far the most important preparation you can do for any negotiation.

Conduct a SWOT Analysis: Prior to entering into a negotiation, it is immensely beneficial to perform a quick SWOT analysis—assessing your strengths, weaknesses, opportunities, and threats—to identify your objectives clearly and strategically. Strengths and weaknesses are internal; opportunities and threats are external. This preparatory step serves as a powerful tool to enhance your understanding of the negotiation landscape, allowing you to approach the table with confidence and clarity. You can do a personal SWOT analysis and a company SWOT analysis. Both are valuable. By evaluating your strengths, you can leverage the unique advantages and assets you bring to the negotiation, using them to bolster your position and influence. Recognizing your weaknesses enables you to be mindful of potential vulnerabilities, preparing you to address them proactively or mitigate their impact. Identifying opportunities helps you pinpoint areas where you can capitalize on favorable conditions or synergies, enhancing the potential for mutually beneficial outcomes. Lastly, understanding potential threats allows you to anticipate challenges and obstacles, equipping you with strategies to navigate or counteract them effectively. This comprehensive analysis not only sharpens your focus on what you aim to achieve but also provides a structured framework to guide your negotiation strategy.

Practice: This may go without saying, but I'm saying it anyway. Practice makes perfect. Don't be overconfident. Even if you've done plenty of presenting in your career, you should still practice, practice, practice. Practice vulnerability and transparency, and you'll find that many others will naturally respond in kind. The more you embrace and embody these qualities, the more they will become second nature, shaping not only your interactions but the person you strive to be.

Role-Play: Even if you've done plenty of presentations before, being part of a negotiating team might be new or unfamiliar. If this is the case, reach out to a seasoned negotiator and do some role-playing. It might feel a little awkward at first, but it will help you learn to navigate surprises and dissension, which are common in negotiations.

Work with a Coach: A good coach with negotiation experience can shorten the learning curve and get you ready for your next negotiation—and future negotiations in general. They can also help you assess and learn from your past negotiations, which is also important. A coach will give important feedback on your people skills and tell you what your strengths and weaknesses are.

Keep a Negotiation Journal: People keep professional journals for all sorts of activities, so why not have a negotiation journal? It gives you the opportunity to capture emotions, feelings, and behaviors in the moment and track your journey over time.

Do the Exercises in This Book: *The Negotiation Code* is packed with exercises to help you become a better negotiator. Take advantage of them and incorporate them into your planning, preparation, and training.

Let me share an example of how these steps and principles can work to build lasting partnerships in the real world. A few years ago, I was part of an acquisition team, and we had some surprises during the negotiations. Everything started out well. We went to see the company's manufacturing facility, which was based in Europe and was quite impressive. We met with the owners and key members of their staff—again very impressive. The acquisition team wanted to buy the company, so we signed an NDA to start our due diligence. When we were reviewing the numbers, we found the company was bringing in an impressive $100 million in gross revenue each year but only generating about $1 million in EBITDA—and they were trying to sell the business for $30 million. The owners were basically asking us to pay a 30x-multiple, which wasn't going to fly.

We could have walked away, but everything else about the business impressed us, so I decided to be honest with them. I set up a meeting with them and told them that they'd never be able to get their asking price without some changes to their business and their bottom line. Because I had earned their trust throughout the course of our negotiation, I offered to advise them for free for a couple of months and share the playbook I use in my board and executive roles to grow their company more profitably. I'd developed my playbook of business strategies over the years by serving on many corporate boards and in C-suite roes. I knew what would work, so I told them exactly what to do. "Call me when it works," I told them, "and we'll come back and take another look at acquiring your business." Only eighteen months later, I got a call from the owner. Not only had his company doubled its revenue, but their EBITDA was now $20 million. The owners were ecstatic and could now get a lot more money for their business. In fact, it was likely their business's value had risen to more than $100 million after only eighteen months of work. This was more than three times what they were originally asking for their business. The owner was ecstatic. Both parties benefitted because neither was shortsighted. Both teams worked together to forge a long-term relationship and create value. None of this would have been possible without the foundation of trust and the strength of a close, genuine relationship. That's the power of effective negotiation!

Conclusion

When you combine clear goals with strong people skills and thoroughly plan and prepare for a negotiation, you demonstrate your commitment to achieving excellence and mutually beneficial outcomes. This allows you to enjoy all the opportunities that accompany this approach—and as the story above demonstrates, the results can be nothing short of spectacular. By unlocking *The Negotiation Code* all of us are capable of unlocking, you've committed to a powerful journey of personal and professional growth that will empower you with confidence, clarity, and wisdom—all of which lead to better outcomes and more value creation.

Notes

_____

_____

_____

_____

_____

_____

_____

_____

_____

_____

_____

_____

_____

_____

_____

_____

_____

_____

_____

_____

_____

_____

_____

_____

_____

_____

_____

_____

_____

_____

_____

_____

_____

_____

_____

_____

_____

_____

_____

_____

_____

_____

_____

_____

_____

_____

ARTIFICIAL
INTELLIGENCE AND
GENERATIVE AI MAY
BE THE MOST
IMPORTANT
TECHNOLOGY OF
ANY LIFETIME.

— *Marc Benioff*

STRATEGY 4

HARNESS ARTIFICIAL INTELLIGENCE

ARTIFICIAL INTELLIGENCE (AI) is no longer confined to data analysis, blog writing, or process automation. It has become an indispensable tool in strategy and, for me, in the negotiation process. Complex negotiations involving multiple parties, interests, and dynamic variables often exceed a negotiator's capacity for real-time processing and analysis. In these situations, AI can serve as a powerful co-negotiator, offering analytical insights, suggesting strategies, and identifying patterns that might otherwise go unnoticed. But AI is only as effective as the instructions or prompts it is given, so the trick is to learn how to harness its full potential. AI is not a replacement for leaders but a tool to augment decision-making, automate processes, and enhance efficiency. As a foundation, this means you need to understand the goals you want to achieve in the negotiation and the role AI will play as your co-negotiator.

AI's Value

At its core, AI excels in the analysis of large data sets and the prediction of potential outcomes. This capability is invaluable in negotiations, where multiple factors—such as economic conditions, historical trends, behavioral biases, and strategic moves—all intersect. AI uses machine learning algorithms and large language models (LLMs) to simulate a range of negotiation outcomes, based on precedents. Based on the AI's findings, it can then provide potential avenues and strategies for a successful outcome. Importantly, AI also reduces human biases, making decision-making more data-driven and logical. For instance, in complex mergers and acquisitions, AI can assess historical mergers, highlight industry trends, and predict how synergies might unfold. By understanding prior market behavior and extrapolating from that data, AI becomes instrumental in creating value from a deal while managing risks.

Furthermore, AI can tap into behavioral economics to model how individuals might react under certain conditions. For example, it can predict potential concessions and counteroffers based on the historical behavior of similar parties in similar types of negotiations. For example, if one party has a history of aiming high in negotiations, AI can suggest appropriate countermeasures. This behavioral aspect of AI brings an additional layer of sophistication to complex negotiations by helping negotiators anticipate emotional responses, biases, and risk-tolerance levels. By offering counterstrategies grounded in behavioral patterns, AI can help negotiators prepare for tricky scenarios that might unfold. And in the heat of a negotiation, when unanticipated scenarios occur, as they so often do, AI can be used to help negotiators react quickly and effectively.

Enhancing Your Edge

As artificial intelligence evolves from a support tool into a strategic partner, negotiators are facing a powerful new reality: AI isn't just helping humans negotiate better—it's learning to negotiate on its own. A recent large-scale negotiation study analyzed over 120,000 AI-driven negotiation simulations. These simulations involved AI agents interacting with both humans and other AI agents across realistic business scenarios—buyer-seller, landlord-tenant, recruiter-candidate, and more. The agents were guided by prompts crafted to reflect different negotiation styles and strategies. The results provided a unique window into what works when AI is in the driver's seat—and what this means for us as leaders using AI to strengthen our own approach. What became clear is this: even without human emotion, AI agents performed best when using emotionally intelligent language. Warmth, empathy, and flexibility produced better outcomes than cold, logic-heavy demands. Strategic communication—especially in the tone of prompts—played a critical role in determining success.

Warmth and Dominance:
The Two Traits that Changed Everything

The study found that AI negotiators performed differently depending on the tone embedded in their instructions. When agents were prompted to express warmth—using phrases like "thank you," "I understand," or "how can we create a win-win?"—they reached more deals and generated higher satisfaction from their counterparts. When agents used dominant language—direct, aggressive, or demand focused—they claimed more value *if* a deal was reached but often failed to reach one at all. Here's the simplified takeaway:

Trait:

- *High Warmth*
  - Higher deal frequency
  - Slightly lower value claimed
  - Higher counterpart satisfaction
- *High Dominance*
  - Lower deal frequency
  - Higher value claimed
  - Lower counterpart satisfaction
- *Combined Warmth and Dominance*
  - Balanced outcomes
  - Moderate satisfaction
  - Deal frequency varied

Warmth helps open doors. Dominance may help close them. The real power lies in the ability to use both and at the right time.

Prompt Engineering:
A Strategic Skill for Modern Negotiators

The simulations revealed it wasn't just tone that mattered but also structure. The most effective AI negotiators used a reasoning process called *chain-of-thought prompting*, where the agent is asked to reason step-by-step before proposing a deal. This mirrors how strong human negotiators prepare: reflect, analyze, anticipate, act.

Here's how to structure a chain-of-thought prompt for your own use:

1. What is the goal in this negotiation?
2. What trade-offs or concessions are acceptable?
3. What does the other party likely care about?
4. What language would make the offer feel respectful and collaborative?

From there, the AI can formulate a proposal. This structure encourages depth, context, and creativity—all key to generating smarter outcomes. Some advanced users also included what's known as *prompt injection*—embedding behavioral values directly into the AI's identity. For example: *You are a negotiator who always seeks common ground and builds trust first. You frame concessions as shared wins, and your tone is warm, respectful, and strategic.* This type of guidance ensures the AI aligns with your leadership style and values—which is especially important when the negotiation stakes are high.

AI as a Copilot for BSO™ and UNO™

This is where frameworks like Best Secondary Options (BSO) and Unified Negotiation Options (UNO) come into play. We'll discuss these in-depth in chapters 8 and 9. By prompting an AI tool to simulate or stress test negotiation packages, leaders can prepare more effectively and uncover value others miss. Here's an example of how to use AI to cocreate your UNO options:

First, create three UNO negotiation packages:
Option A: High pricing, high value-added services.
Option B: Balanced pricing, expedited delivery.
Option C: Discounted pricing, no support services.

Each option should be:
- Anchored in value.
- Warm in tone.
- Structured with clear trade-offs and built-in concessions.
- Designed to feel generous and strategic to the other party.

You can also use the AI to sharpen your BSO by using prompts like this: "Assume the deal falls through. Based on my fallback plan, what other options could I strengthen to increase my leverage? What objections might I face? How could I reframe them?" By partnering with AI in this way, you're not delegating the thinking—you're sharpening your edge. You're using the tool to challenge your thinking, expand your creativity, and uncover blind spots before they cost you.

Limitations

AI is not without its limitations. While it processes data and suggests optimal paths, it does not yet possess human intuition, empathy, or emotional intelligence—traits that are crucial in any negotiation. In other words, it does not have people skills or the ability to build trust or relationships. Reading nonverbal cues, seeing cultural nuances, and building relationships are outside the scope of AI's current capabilities. Moreover, AI lacks moral judgment, and this can sometimes result in recommendations that, while strategically sound, may be ethically questionable. Furthermore, AI tends to "hallucinate" and needs constant checking. This is why AI should be seen as a tool that complements human negotiation rather than replaces it.

Effective Prompts

Using AI in a negotiation without knowing how to craft effective prompts is useless. Generic prompts produce generic answers from AI. Well-crafted prompts are what make AI an effective negotiation tool. Prompting AI effectively is as much an art as it is a science. The quality of AI output is directly related to how well a prompt is structured. In the context of negotiations, providing clear, detailed, and nuanced prompts is crucial for receiving useful and actionable insights and guidance. We'll explore how to create an effective prompt later in the chapter.

Goals and Objectives

Before engaging with AI, it's essential to define clear goals and objectives for the negotiation. Are you aiming to close a deal? Secure concessions? Build a long-term partnership? Something else? Your answers matter. We'll discuss this in-depth in the next strategy, but for the purposes of AI prompting, different goals and objectives should influence your interaction with AI. For example, if the objective is to secure a fair price in a transaction, you might prompt the AI as follows: *I am negotiating a purchase agreement for industrial equipment. Our target price is $5 million, but the seller is asking for $6.5 million. What strategies can I use to close* *the deal at a fair price while maintaining a strong relationship with the seller?* This prompt provides clear direction for the AI to focus on pricing strategies while considering relationship dynamics. However, it doesn't stop there. This is just the beginning of your conversation.

Context and Background

AI performs best when it understands the full context of a situation, its role, and what exactly you're looking for. It is essential to provide background information on the parties involved, any previous interactions, industry standards, and any relevant market or regulatory conditions. Without sufficient context, AI may offer generic advice that lacks specificity. Here's an example of an effective prompt and the response ChatGPT produced:

> AI Prompt: *We are in the final stages of negotiating a merger between a midsize biotech firm and a large pharmaceutical company. The biotech firm holds several patents on innovative drug treatments, while the pharmaceutical company brings substantial manufacturing and distribution capabilities. We are struggling to agree on intellectual property ownership post-merger. What strategies can we use to resolve this issue while ensuring a mutually beneficial agreement?*
>
> AI Response: *To resolve the intellectual property ownership issue while ensuring a mutually beneficial agreement in the merger, consider these strategies:*

Joint Ownership and Licensing

- Create a joint ownership model where the intellectual property (IP) remains under the shared control of both parties.
- The pharmaceutical company can license the biotech firm's patents for manufacturing and distribution, with royalties or revenue-sharing arrangements in place.

Segmentation of IP Rights

- Divide the IP by its application or geographic region. For example:
    - The biotech firm retains rights for research and development.
    - The pharmaceutical company gains rights for manufacturing, marketing, and sales in a specific region.

Establish a New Entity for IP Management

- Form a separate entity or division to manage the IP, with ownership and decision-making shared proportionally.
- This entity would handle licensing, litigation, and innovation extensions collaboratively.

Performance-Based Escalation Clauses

- Tie IP ownership to performance metrics or milestones post-merger.
- If the pharmaceutical company meets certain sales or investment thresholds, additional rights or ownership percentages could be transferred.

Royalty Structures

- *Develop a tiered royalty agreement where the biotech firm retains ownership of the IP but allows the pharmaceutical company exclusive use for agreed terms, with ongoing payments.*

Future Development Agreements

- *Maintain the biotech firm as a separate R&D unit under the merged organization.*
- *The biotech team continues to innovate under its name, with shared profits or ownership of new discoveries.*

Neutral Third-Party Mediation

- *Engage a neutral third party (e.g., legal or financial experts) to mediate the negotiation.*
- *Their role would be to ensure fair valuation of the IP and propose balanced solutions for ownership.*

Valuation-Based Equity Exchange

- *Conduct an independent valuation of the biotech firm's IP portfolio.*
- *Use this valuation to adjust the equity split or financial terms of the merger.*

For a well-prepared negotiator, an effective prompt should take only a couple of minutes to craft. And, of course, AI's answer took only seconds yet represents what might have taken hours of human research and thought. This is the power of AI when it's properly prompted.

Iterative Prompting

One of the most powerful aspects of using AI in negotiations is the ability to engage in a dialogue, allowing you to refine and iterate on responses. This process of iterative prompting helps negotiators arrive at more precise ideas and strategies. Initial responses from AI may be general and broad. Follow-up prompts can drill down into specific details. For example, you can ask for further clarification or exploration of one of the options provided in the previous prompt. A follow-up prompt might look like this: *Could you elaborate on how a joint intellectual property ownership model might work in this context? What risks should we be aware of, and how can we mitigate them?* The AI will then refine its advice, making it more actionable and relevant to the situation at hand. In the case of the above prompt, ChatGPT completed its follow-up answer by asking, *Would you like help refining these strategies or applying them to your specific context?* I could have replied yes and received additional details and ideas about how to handle negotiation challenges.

One advanced technique to improve AI responses is chain-of-thought prompting. This involves asking the AI to think through a problem step-by-step, breaking it down into smaller components rather than expecting a fully formed answer immediately. For example, instead of asking, *What are the best strategies for this negotiation?* you might prompt the AI to first list possible goals, then identify potential obstacles, and finally propose strategies tailored to overcoming those obstacles. By guiding the AI's reasoning process, you can uncover insights that might otherwise be overlooked. You're able to ask the AI to keep everything the same, but change *x*, *y*, or *z*. Also, you can tell it to commit certain information to memory for the next time you're working with it on this subject.

Ethical and Bias Filters

While incredibly efficient, AI can reflect biases present in its training data. It's crucial to account for this by explicitly instructing the AI to recognize and mitigate potential biases in the advice it provides. For example, AI might suggest aggressive strategies that could strain long-term relationships with a business partner or favor one party over another. To counter this, include ethical considerations in your prompts. Here's how this might look: *While considering an aggressive negotiation strategy to secure intellectual property rights, how can we ensure the approach remains ethical and maintains a good working relationship post-merger?* This ensures the AI's output aligns not just with your immediate strategic goals in the negotiation but with ethical considerations and longer-term goals.

Real-World Example: Complex Corporate Merger

Let's dive into a real-world example where AI assists in a complex corporate merger between a midsize healthcare company and a large multinational corporation. The midsize healthcare company is highly innovative, owning several patents for breakthrough treatments. The multinational corporation, however, offers vast distribution networks, regulatory expertise, and the financial capital necessary to scale the healthcare company's products globally. I used ChatGPT to explore the key negotiation issues, which included:

- Intellectual property control and the division of royalties post-merger.
- Retention and incentivization of the healthcare company's leadership.
- A profit-sharing mechanism based on geographical market performance.
- Long-term operational synergies around research and development teams.

AI Prompt: *I'm negotiating a merger between a midsize healthcare company with strong IP assets and a multinational corporation. Our key issues are IP ownership post-merger, leadership retention, profit-sharing mechanisms in emerging markets, and operational synergies. What strategies can I use to ensure a fair and mutually beneficial agreement?*

AI Response: *Here are targeted strategies to address each key issue in your merger negotiations, ensuring a fair and mutually beneficial agreement:*

IP Ownership Post-Merger
- *Hybrid Ownership Model: Split ownership based on functionality:*
  - *Healthcare Company: Retains ownership of existing IP related to innovation and R&D.*
  - *Multinational Corporation: Gains exclusive rights for manufacturing, marketing, and distribution.*
- *Performance-Based Ownership: Ownership transfer is tied to predefined performance milestones, ensuring value alignment.*

- *New IP Entity: Establish a jointly owned subsidiary to manage IP, with profit sharing proportional to contributions and usage rights.*

Leadership Retention
- *Retention Packages: Offer tailored incentives such as:*
  - ○ *Equity stakes in the merged entity.*
  - ○ *Retention bonuses tied to tenure or performance.*
- *Strategic Roles: Ensure key leaders from the healthcare company are retained in critical decision-making roles to preserve institutional knowledge and IP expertise.*
- *Joint Leadership Framework: Integrate leaders into a dual management structure to oversee critical areas (e.g., R&D, operations).*

Profit-Sharing Mechanisms in Emerging Markets
- *Region-Specific Profit-Sharing Models:*
  - ○ *Base profit-sharing ratios on market penetration goals and investment levels by each party.*
- *Tiered Revenue Sharing:*
  - ○ *Initially, have higher revenue shares for the healthcare company to offset IP value.*
  - ○ *Adjust shares as the multinational corporation invests in scaling operations.*
- *Joint Ventures: Establish regional joint ventures for emerging markets, ensuring shared risks and rewards.*

Operational Synergies
- *Integration Planning:*
    - Conduct a detailed synergy assessment to identify cost-saving opportunities in supply chain, R&D, and production.
    - Assign teams from both entities to oversee integration in key areas.
- *Resource Sharing Agreements:*
    - The multinational corporation can leverage its global distribution network.
    - The healthcare company focuses on advancing IP and innovation pipelines.
- *Shared Innovation Hubs:*
    - Create comanaged innovation hubs to optimize resource allocation and foster collaboration.

Overarching Strategies
- *Valuation and Transparency:*
    - Conduct an independent valuation of IP, leadership assets, and market opportunities to establish a fair baseline.
    - Share findings with both parties to build trust.
- *Neutral Mediator:*
    - Engage a third-party mediator or advisor to help resolve contentious issues like IP ownership and profit sharing.
- *Milestone-Based Agreements:*
    - Use a phased approach for IP transfer, leadership integration, and profit sharing tied to measurable outcomes (e.g., revenue growth, market entry).

- *Governance Structure:*
  - ° *Define a clear governance framework for decision-making post-merger, balancing representation from both companies.*
- *Cultural Integration Plan:*
  - ° *Address potential cultural differences between the healthcare company's innovation-driven approach and the multinational's operational focus.*

Would you like a more detailed draft of any of these frameworks, or assistance structuring the negotiation process for specific issues?

After receiving these initial AI recommendations, you'll note that it's asking if I'd like more detail. You always want to explore these follow-up prompts. However, they can sometimes be high-level, when you might be looking for detail. That's why it's important to iterate on your initial prompts to further refine specific insights. This is when AI shines as an effective tool for your negotiation strategy. In this case, I wanted deeper analysis on the staggered IP-sharing model that ChatGPT had suggested.

My AI Follow-Up Prompt: *Can you provide a deeper analysis on the staggered IP-sharing model, especially how it can be structured to balance risk for both parties?*

AI's Answer: *A staggered IP-sharing model is an excellent way to balance risks and ensure fair value exchange between the healthcare company and the multinational corporation. Below is a deeper analysis of how this model can be structured:*

Core Components of the Staggered IP-Sharing Model

1. *Phased Transfer of Ownership or Usage Rights*

- ○ *IP ownership or usage rights are transferred in stages, tied to predefined milestones.*
- ○ **Ownership Phases:**
  - ▪ **Phase 1:** *Initial licensing for limited applications or geographies.*
  - ▪ **Phase 2:** *Joint ownership upon achieving milestones (e.g., revenue or production targets).*
  - ▪ **Phase 3:** *Full ownership by the multinational corporation based on agreed-upon terms.*

2. *Performance-Based Triggers*

- ○ *Define clear, measurable triggers for each phase:*
  - ▪ *Revenue benchmarks (e.g., $X million in sales from IP-derived products).*
  - ▪ *Market entry goals (e.g., successful entry into Y emerging markets).*
  - ▪ *R&D milestones (e.g., development of next-generation IP).*

3. *Revenue Sharing*

- ○ *Establish tiered royalty or revenue-sharing arrangements:*
  - ▪ **Initial Phase:** *Higher royalties to the healthcare company, reflecting the risk and up-front IP investment.*

- **Later Phases:** Reduced royalties as the multinational scales production and distribution.

4. IP Valuation and Equity Adjustments

- Conduct an independent valuation of the IP portfolio up front.
- Structure the merger with equity adjustments based on the realization of IP-related value during the staggered phases.

Risk-Balancing Mechanisms

1. For the Healthcare Company

- **Risk:** Loss of IP control and long-term value dilution.
- **Mitigation:**
  - Retain veto rights over IP licensing or modification during the early phases.
  - Embed clawback clauses allowing reversion of rights if milestones are unmet.

2. For the Multinational Corporation

- **Risk:** Uncertainty in IP scalability and profitability.
- **Mitigation:**
  - Begin with exclusive licensing rather than ownership to limit initial financial exposure.
  - Require the healthcare company to provide technical support and expertise during initial scaling.

3. Shared Risk Mitigation

- Use an escrow mechanism for financial or IP transfer commitments.
- Create a dispute resolution process to handle milestone disagreements.

Governance and Operationalization

1. Joint Governance Committee

- Set up a committee with representatives from both companies to oversee milestone achievement and enforce phased agreements.

2. Technology Transfer Support

- The healthcare company provides expertise and technical assistance during the early stages of IP commercialization.

3. Regular Reviews

- Conduct quarterly or semiannual reviews to assess progress against milestones and adjust terms if necessary.

Advantages of Staggered IP Sharing

1. **Flexibility:** Allows both parties to test the waters and refine the partnership dynamically.
2. **Risk Distribution:** Distributes risk proportionally based on milestones rather than placing a heavy burden on one party.

3. ***Incentive Alignment:*** *Encourages both parties to maximize the value of the IP through shared success metrics.*

Would you like assistance in drafting specific agreements or evaluating financial scenarios for this model?

Illustrative Structure of the Staggered IP-Sharing Model

Phase	Ownership/ Usage	Revenue Sharing	Key Milestone
Phase 1	Exclusive license	15% royalties to healthcare	First $50M in IP-derived revenue
Phase 2	Joint ownership	10% royalties to healthcare	Market entry into 3 new regions
Phase 3	Full ownership	5% royalties to healthcare	$200M cumulative revenue achieved

Not only are the AI's insights nearly instantaneous, but the quality of this reply is impressive. Notice that it's offering to draft agreements, which takes things to an entirely new level. Hopefully, this real-world example provides a basic model for all types of negotiations and situations. Learning how to harness the power of AI takes time and practice but is definitely worth the effort. In fact, with the speed at which AI is learning and being adopted into the negotiating process, it is becoming an indispensable negotiation tool that business leaders ignore at their peril.

Structure Your Approach

A structured, intentional approach to AI prompting, using AI as a thought leader, will unlock its full potential, yielding deeper insights and a more robust selection of solutions from which to choose. Consider these six techniques for optimizing AI's role in the negotiating process:

1. **Assign a Role:** Within your prompts, assign the AI a specific role inside or outside your negotiation. For instance, as part of your prompt, you might say: *You are a strategic consultant tasked with maximizing my company's leverage while ensuring a mutually beneficial outcome for both parties.* Giving the AI a clear role creates a more focused interaction that aligns with your overall goals for the negotiation and what knowledge you'd like it to draw from. You could ask it to act as a challenger, collaborator, or strategist, depending on your needs.

2. **Encourage Clarifying Questions**: The best AI responses are often a product of clear and comprehensive information. Encourage the AI to ask you clarifying questions if anything is ambiguous or missing from the initial prompt. This "dialogue" can sharpen the AI's understanding of specific elements of a negotiation and lead to more tailored, relevant strategies. For example, if you're negotiating a merger and you tell the AI to ask you clarifying questions, it might ask: *What are the key motivations for both parties? Are there any*

nonnegotiable points? What are the risks and bene-fits of this approach? What assumptions am I mak-ing that could be wrong? Answering such questions can help the AI refine its responses and help you think through negotiating tactics you might not have considered yet.

3. **Request "Nonobvious" Suggestions**: Push beyond surface-level advice by specifically asking the AI to generate nonobvious solutions. This encourages the AI to tap into less conventional strategies and insights that might not emerge through traditional negotiation frameworks. For example, instead of focusing solely on financial terms during a merger negotiation, the AI could suggest innovative incen-tives like phased IP sharing or profit sharing tied to performance metrics. Requesting nonobvious suggestions from AI can broaden your choices and alert you to novel negotiating strategies.

4. **Prompt for Multiple Perspectives**: Often, AI can be biased toward the perspectives that you pro-vide. To avoid this, and to generate more com-prehensive and less biased responses, prompt the AI to explore every subject from multiple angles. For instance, you could prompt the AI in this way: *Provide the potential concerns from the opposing party's perspective, then suggest a strategy that bal-ances both interests.* This multifaceted approach ensures you're not overlooking critical perspec-tives that might surface during a negotiation.

5. **Layer Your Prompts**: AI can generate more refined answers when it is prompted in stages.

Start with prompts that are specific but ask for a high-level overview. Then, gradually drill down into specific elements. For example, after receiving the AI's initial advice on a negotiation strategy, follow up with more detailed prompts. Here are some examples: *How would this approach be impacted if regulatory constraints were introduced? What concessions could we offer without weakening our core position? Can you expand on point X? What other factors should I consider here? Which of these factors should I focus on first, and why?*

Test AI's Suggestions

Before relying on any of AI's recommendations, prompt the AI to consider the potential downsides or vulnerabilities of its own solutions. For instance, you could ask: *What are the potential risks or unintended consequences of this approach?* This creates an opportunity to evaluate the robustness of the AI's suggestions, helps you anticipate countermoves, and serves as a quality check. It is important to remember that AI does make mistakes, despite all its power. AI is a wonderful idea and solutions generator, but it is always important to independently verify all facts, data, and insights that it provides.

Train Your AI Persona Prompt

Many people don't realize they can *train* their AI tool to align with their leadership style. Treat AI like a values-aligned copilot.

Example Prompt:

You are my negotiation partner. You are insightful, calm, and values driven. You frame deals with empathy and always look for long-term wins over short-term wins. You act as my EQ-optimized sounding board, not a bulldozer. Commit this to your memory for all negotiations I am involved in.

Cross-Reference Future Tools

Briefly flag where AI can assist again in later strategies, such as:

- Crafting a unique value proposition (Strategy 5)
- Simulating counter party framing (Strategy 8)
- Testing your BSO™ logic through worst-case and best-case scenarios (Strategy 8)
- Presenting UNO™ offers with tailored concessions (Strategy 10)

This reinforces the idea that AI isn't a one-and-done tool—it can be integrated across your entire system.

The Road Ahead

The future of negotiation won't be defined by who has the best tactics; it will be shaped by who can best blend emotional intelligence with digital fluency. AI will increasingly take the lead in structured negotiation environments, from vendor contracts to employment offers. But what will separate the excellent from the average is how leaders guide these tools.

We still need vision. We still need empathy. We still need intention. The strongest negotiators will not be replaced by AI. They will become stronger with it. That's what this chapter—and this entire book—is about: not keeping up with the future but shaping it.

Conclusion

AI-driven prompting is transforming the way complex negotiations are approached. By leveraging AI's analytical capabilities, negotiators can anticipate risks, strategize with more precision, and address challenges that arise in real time. However, it's vital to remember that AI serves as a complement to human intuition, emotional intelligence, and judgment. As a negotiator, you first need to become proficient in these key human skills, which still drive successful negotiations. Together, AI and human intelligence create a powerful partnership that offers substantial advantages to negotiators who learn how to effectively tailor the immense power of AI to their specific negotiating needs. This means not only having a structured approach to AI usage but also staying abreast of the latest innovations in AI, which are constant. If you follow this guidance, AI will become an invaluable co-negotiator that will help you secure better outcomes even in the most complex negotiation scenarios.

Notes

_____

_____

_____

_____

_____

_____

_____

_____

_____

_____

_____

_____

IT'S NOT
WHAT YOU
SELL THAT
MATTERS AS
MUCH AS
HOW YOU
SELL IT.

— *Brian Halligan*

CRAFT A UNIQUE VALUE PROPOSITION

IN A CROWDED marketplace, what truly sets negotiators apart is their unique value proposition—those singular strengths, capabilities, ideas, and achievements that differentiate them. As part of the preparation and planning stage, you should document what makes you, your company, and your offering exceptional. This will not only give you confidence as you enter a negotiation, it will also prepare you to clearly articulate your offer's distinctive elements when the moment arises. You'll be ready to show how your unique value proposition addresses the needs and challenges of the other party and offer a compelling case for why partnering with you is the best choice. By effectively communicating what makes your offer indispensable, you build trust and demonstrate your commitment to delivering exceptional results. Embrace your unique value proposition as a cornerstone of your negotiation strategy.

As discussed in the negotiation basics section at the beginning of this book, conducting a comprehensive SWOT analysis is foundational to the negotiation process.

You should definitely have your SWOT analysis completed before working on your unique value proposition. As a reminder, an effective SWOT analysis meticulously identifies your unique strengths and weaknesses as well as the external opportunities and threats relevant to you. This thoughtful and strategic process is essential for understanding and leveraging your unique position in the marketplace. Now, you are ready for Strategy 5.

Explore Your Unique Selling Points

Unique selling points (USPs) are the defining attributes that serve as the cornerstone of your value proposition. By emphasizing your USPs, you demonstrate a deep understanding of the value you bring, reinforcing your credibility and inspiring trust. This fosters a sense of respect and admiration. Whenever possible, seize the opportunity during a negotiation to demonstrate your USPs through compelling examples of past performance. Storytelling and case studies are both excellent tools for this. Leverage endorsements and praise from respected third parties—industry experts, satisfied clients, prestigious award panels, etc. These independent affirmations add credibility and reinforce your reputation as a trusted and capable partner. Stay humble when you share all these with negotiating partners, making sure to acknowledge that your successes are the result of collaborative efforts, continuous learning, and a steadfast commitment to excellence.

Highlight Your Experience and Network

USPs often go beyond finances. In any negotiation, you should have a list of intangibles. Don't shy away from highlighting your extensive industry or general business experience as a significant and special advantage. Emphasize how your comprehensive insights, honed over many years, enable you to predict market changes with greater precision and accuracy. This level of foresight not only sets you apart but allows you to add lasting value to your partnerships. Share specific examples of how your extensive background has equipped you to navigate complex challenges, anticipate industry shifts, and implement innovative solutions that drive success. Approach this discussion with humility by recognizing that your expertise is the result of continuous learning, dedication, and a genuine passion for the field. By illustrating how your seasoned perspective enhances your ability to deliver exceptional results, you build trust and confidence with potential partners. Explain how your unique vantage point enables you to offer strategic guidance and informed decision-making that can significantly benefit their organization. This not only underscores your value proposition but demonstrates your commitment to leveraging your experience for their success. Through this narrative, you inspire confidence and convey a sense of reliability and excellence, positioning yourself as a trusted advisor dedicated to making a meaningful and enduring impact in the industry.

Analyzing USPs with a Venn Diagram

A Venn diagram is a visual tool used to illustrate the relationships between different sets of items. In the context of negotiations, a Venn diagram can be incredibly useful for comparing your unique selling points (USPs) with those of your competitors. This comparison helps to clarify where your offerings overlap with competitors and, more importantly, where you are unique—those aspects only you can provide. Here's how to create and use a Venn diagram:

Identify Key USPs: Begin by listing all the unique features, strengths, and advantages you and your competitors offer. This could include superior customer service, innovative technology, industry experience, or financial stability,

Draw the Diagram: The Venn diagram typically consists of two or more overlapping circles. Each circle represents a different competitor or entity, including yourself. The overlapping areas show the common features shared by you and your competitors, while the nonoverlapping areas highlight what is unique to each.

Analyze Overlaps and Uniqueness: The areas where your circle overlaps with those of competitors represent features that are not entirely unique to you but are still important. While these might not set you apart, they are critical to maintaining parity in the market. The areas of your circle that do not overlap with others are your true USPs—these are the features or benefits that only you can provide. This is where your strength lies in the negotiation, as you can emphasize these unique qualities to demonstrate why you are the best choice. It's essential to focus on what truly sets you apart in the eyes of others, rather than solely relying on what you believe makes you unique.

Your uniqueness is defined entirely by how others perceive it.

Strategic Application: Use the diagram during negotiations to visually show the other party where you stand out. This helps them to quickly grasp the value you bring to the table that no other competitor can offer. It also helps you to strategically position yourself, ensuring your unique advantages are clearly communicated and understood.

YOUR USPs AND COMPETITORS' USPs
BREAKDOWN

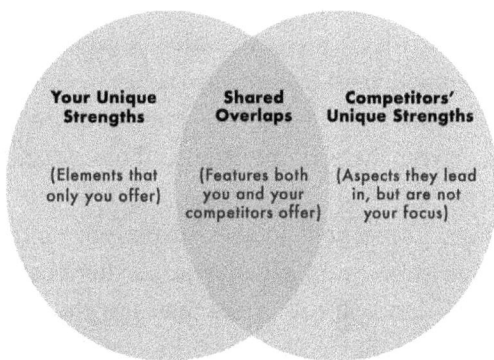

Your Unique Strengths	Shared Overlaps	Competitors' Unique Strengths
(Elements that only you offer)	(Features both you and your competitors offer)	(Aspects they lead in, but are not your focus)

The chart continues through to "Proposal Presentation," where you showcase your integrated service platform that offers unmatched scalability.

Finally, the chart includes "Agreement Finalization," where your track record of successful long-term partnerships is emphasized. This chart not only keeps the negotiation on track but ensures the other party fully understands the comprehensive value you offer.

Maybe your superpower is cultivating long-term relationships built on trust, collaboration, and mutual growth. These enduring partnerships create a solid foundation for ongoing success, where both parties can thrive and innovate together. As a result, you might have an expansive network of connections you bring to the negotiating table, and you can offer access to the other party. Make sure you know how to present this as the key to opening doors to new opportunities, strategic alliances, and potential clients that can significantly enhance the other party's business. Your industry experience and network is an invaluable asset. Don't sell it short. And remember, the true impact lies in action. Open a meaningful door or two for them—opportunities significant enough to leave a lasting impression and make them eager to engage further.

By highlighting your industry experience and extensive network, you show your negotiating partner that by aligning with you, they will gain more than just the benefits of a business transaction; they also will be entering into a valuable partnership with intangible fringe benefits. Embrace this holistic perspective during negotiations and make sure to convey how your unique blend of relationship building, networking, and industry expertise makes you an indispensable ally. You transform from just another party at the table into a true partner in the process. This not only strengthens your negotiation stance but also inspires confidence and enthusiasm, paving the way for a fruitful and lasting collaboration. Here are some USPs worth exploring when you are planning for a negotiation:

Irreplaceability: Reflect on what you provide that can't easily be found elsewhere. This can give you significant leverage in negotiations. Consider the exceptional qualities and distinctive advantages that make you, your services, or products truly one of a kind. Whether it's proprietary technology, unparalleled expertise, personalized customer service, or a proven track record of delivering exceptional results, these unique attributes set you apart in a competitive landscape. Emphasize how your offering addresses specific challenges and meets needs in ways others simply cannot. This not only showcases your distinctiveness but highlights your commitment to excellence and innovation. Approach this USP with humility, recognizing that your uniqueness is a result of dedication, hard work, and a deep understanding of your field. Your distinctiveness can provide leverage to negotiate from a position of strength while fostering a collaborative spirit. Ultimately, irreplaceability is not just a selling point but a testament to the exceptional value you bring, inspiring confidence and paving the way for a successful and mutually beneficial partnership.

Financial Stability: Emphasize your strong financial health as a cornerstone of your unique value proposition, showcasing your unwavering reliability as a long-term business partner. By presenting clear and transparent evidence of your financial stability, you instill confidence and trust, reassuring potential partners that you are well-equipped to navigate economic fluctuations and sustain your commitments over the long haul. Share financial results in percentages, credit ratings, or independent assessments that underscore your robust financial position. Highlighting your fiscal responsibility not only sets you apart from competitors but demonstrates your prudent management and strategic foresight. Approach this discussion with humility, acknowledging that your financial strength is a result of disciplined practices, effective leadership, and a commitment to sustainable growth. By underscoring these attributes, you affirm your capability to support significant projects, invest in innovative solutions, and provide consistent, high-quality service. This level of transparency and reliability reinforces your reputation as a trustworthy and dependable partner, dedicated to fostering enduring relationships and mutual success. This in turn paves the way for robust, collaborative negotiations and partnerships built on a foundation of trust and shared goals.

High Client Satisfaction: Use specific, compelling data to demonstrate elevated levels of customer contentment and quicker service times, illustrating how you consistently exceed basic expectations. Share quantifiable metrics—such as customer satisfaction scores, testimonials, and service benchmarks—to provide a clear and persuasive picture of your superior performance. Highlight how these achievements reflect your unwavering commitment to excellence and your relentless drive to deliver exceptional value. During this discussion, it's important to acknowledge that these accomplishments are the result of a dedicated team effort, continuous improvement, and a deep understanding of customer needs. This not only builds trust and credibility but inspires confidence in your ability to deliver outstanding results. Emphasize how your focus on exceeding expectations leads to meaningful, positive impacts for your clients, whether it's through enhancing their operational efficiency, improving their customer experiences, or driving their business growth. This approach demonstrates you are not just meeting standards but setting new ones, positioning yourself as a forward-thinking partner dedicated to their success. Always provide references who are not only willing but eager to share their positive experiences working with you. Through this narrative, you highlight your commitment to going above and beyond, fostering a sense of trust and enthusiasm that paves the way for strong, long-term partnerships.

Tailored Solutions: If applicable, highlight your company's remarkable ability to tailor products or services to meet the unique needs of each client, showcasing this as a testament to your commitment to personalized excellence. Emphasize how your customized approaches have consistently led to improved outcomes, and back this up with data and compelling case studies. Share stories of clients who have benefited from your adaptable solutions, illustrating how you have addressed their distinct challenges and helped them achieve their goals. By presenting concrete evidence of your adaptability and the positive impact it has had, you build trust and demonstrate your capability to deliver exceptional, tailored results. Emphasize how this flexibility sets you apart from competitors, showcasing your willingness to go the extra mile to ensure client satisfaction and success. By highlighting your track record of customization and the tangible benefits it brings, you position yourself as a responsive, client-focused partner committed to driving sustained, impactful outcomes for those you serve.

Network Advantages: If you have cultivated strong relationships with people over the years, highlight your role as a strategic connector. Emphasize how partnering could create new opportunities for both of you. Your role as a strategic connector shouldn't be a boast but serve as a testament to your dedication to building meaningful, collaborative relationships that benefit everyone involved. Explain how your network can provide unique insights, resources, and opportunities. Approach this discussion with a genuine desire to collaborate to build a strong and meaningful reputation together. When done right, this means that people want to work with you simply because of who you are. Share specific examples of how past collaborations have led to mutually beneficial outcomes. This positions you as someone who invests in the long-term success of their partners, creating a ripple effect of positive outcomes for everyone involved.

Technology Edge: If your firm prioritizes research and development (R&D) and innovation, explain how your commitments in this area grant you a technological advantage. Highlight your relentless pursuit of cutting-edge advancements and groundbreaking solutions, underscoring how this dedication drives your ability to stay ahead of trends and address evolving client needs. Share specific examples of innovative projects and breakthroughs that have set you apart, illustrating the tangible impact of your R&D efforts. Emphasize how your focus on innovation not only enhances your offerings but creates significant value for your clients, enabling them to achieve their goals more efficiently and effectively. By showcasing the unique technological edge your R&D initiatives provide, you build trust and inspire confidence that you will deliver exceptional, forward-thinking solutions. This narrative not only highlights your unique strengths but also demonstrates your commitment to pushing the boundaries of what is possible, fostering a culture of excellence and inspiring others to join you on the journey of innovation and growth. This positions you as a leader and a visionary partner dedicated to creating lasting impact and driving mutual success through innovation.

Purpose-Driven Impact: If you are deeply committed to creating a positive impact, whether through philanthropy, community engagement, or sustainability initiatives, take pride in sharing this integral aspect of your identity. Highlight how your dedication to giving back reflects a genuine desire to support meaningful causes and drive societal change. Share stories of how your contributions have transformed lives or communities. Provide specific examples of initiatives, partnerships, or measurable outcomes that demonstrate the real-world difference you are making. By weaving this narrative into your negotiations, you position yourself as a partner in progress, a force for good, and someone whom others are proud to support and collaborate with. Your commitment to giving back not only sets you apart but also inspires trust, loyalty, and admiration among clients, employees, and the broader community. Through this message, you demonstrate that success isn't just measured in numbers but in the meaningful and lasting contributions you make to the world.

Create a Flowchart of Your Value Proposition

To prepare to demonstrate your unique value proposition, a flowchart can be useful. This is a step-by-step personal or internal visual representation that outlines a process or a sequence of events. In negotiations, a flowchart of your value proposition can be a powerful tool to visualize how your unique selling points align with the negotiation process to achieve mutual goals. It helps you, and in turn the other party, see the logical progression from the initial engagement to the final agreement, ensuring every step is strategically aligned with your core strengths and objectives. Here's how to create and use the flowchart:

1. **Define Your Value Proposition:** This is the overall promise of value you deliver to your client. This should include your key USPs and how they solve specific problems or meet the needs of the other party.

2. **Map Out the Negotiation Process:** Identify the key stages of the negotiation process. This could include initial contact, understanding the client's needs, presenting your proposal, handling objections, and finalizing the agreement.

3. **Align USPs with Each Stage:** For each stage of the negotiation, identify which of your USPs is most relevant and how it can be leveraged. For example, in the "Understanding the Client's Needs" stage, your USP might be your deep industry knowledge, which allows you to ask insightful questions and fully understand their challenges. In the "Presenting Your Proposal" stage, your USP might be a proprietary technology no one else offers, which you present as the ideal solution.

4. **Visualize the Process**: The flowchart should start with the initiation of the negotiation and move through each stage in a logical sequence. Each stage should be linked by arrows or lines, showing the progression from one step to the next. At each step, note the specific USP that aligns with that stage and how it drives the process forward.

5. **Use Your Flowchart:** Keep referring to the flowchart during negotiations to guide discussions. It serves as a road map for you, ensuring you consistently highlight your unique strengths at the most opportune moments. The visual flow helps you explain to the other party how your value proposition evolves throughout the negotiation, leading them toward a conclusion that your offering is the best solution.

Negotiation Preparation Steps

Step 1: Research the Other Party
- ☐ Identify their goals, interests, and pressures.
- ☐ Analyze their past negotiation behaviors and decision patterns.
- ☐ Research their financial position, industry trends, and competitors.
- ☐ Understand their cultural or organizational nuances.

Step 2: Identify Key Deal Points
- ☐ Define your primary objectives and success criteria. Calculate your BSO and estimate their BSO.
- ☐ Determine critical deal terms (pricing, contract length, deliverables, etc.).
- ☐ Map out what is nonnegotiable vs. flexible. Determine your ambitious goal.
- ☐ Establish potential win-win solutions.

Step 3: Anticipate Objections & Roadblocks
- ☐ List potential pushbacks or concerns from the other party.
- ☐ Prepare counterarguments backed by logic, data, or precedent.
- ☐ Identify emotional triggers or biases that may arise.
- ☐ Have alternative options ready in case certain terms are rejected.

Step 4: Structure Concessions & Trade-Offs
- ☐ Define your opening position and justifications. Is it reasonable?
- ☐ Complete your Negotiation Grid. Decide which concessions you can afford to give without losing leverage.

- [ ] Align trade-offs strategically with your Unified Negotiation Options (UNO) Matrix.
- [ ] Set your BSO to prevent compromising too much.

Make Them Realize What They'll Miss

When framing conversations, consider the principle of loss aversion, as people are often more motivated to avoid potential losses than to pursue equivalent gains. This is also known as fear of missing out (FOMO). By empathetically highlighting what they stand to lose by not taking action, you can effectively underscore the importance and urgency of your proposal. Approach this strategy with sensitivity and respect, making sure the emphasis is on genuinely helping them avoid negative outcomes rather than employing fear tactics.

Illustrate the potential risks and missed opportunities with real-world examples and data, making it clear how your solution can safeguard against these pitfalls. By doing so, you not only address their concerns but build a compelling case for the value and necessity of your offerings. This approach demonstrates your understanding of their priorities and your commitment to protecting their interests. The goal is to inspire action by highlighting the security and benefits your proposal provides, fostering a sense of reassurance and trust. By framing the conversation in this way, you not only motivate them to move forward but establish yourself as a thoughtful and proactive partner dedicated to their success and well-being. In every negotiation, you're not merely selling a product, a service, or specific terms—you're representing yourself and showcasing the values, dedication, and unique strengths that define you. Understand that each interaction in a negotiation is an opportunity to convey your passion, commitment to excellence, and the distinct qualities that set you apart from the competition.

Craft a Narrative That Drives Action

How you position your message in negotiations directly impacts how it is received. Great negotiators don't just present facts—they craft narratives that shape perceptions. Here's how to refine your messaging and positioning:

1. **Make It About Them**
   Frame your proposal in terms of their needs, goals, and challenges rather than just your own.

2. **Use the Right Language**
   Shift from transactional language (e.g., "We need X from you") to collaborative language (e.g., "Here's how we can both benefit").

3. **Reframe Objections**
   Instead of countering resistance directly, reposition objections as opportunities to find solutions together.

4. **Control the First Impression**
   The way you introduce a negotiation **sets the tone**. Ensure your messaging highlights **shared interests** rather than conflicting demands.

By fine-tuning your messaging and positioning, you **guide the conversation toward the outcomes you want while reinforcing alignment and trust.**

Conclusion

By emphasizing your unique value proposition, whether it's unparalleled expertise, innovative solutions, exceptional customer service, or a proven track record of success, you build trust and inspire confidence in your counterpart. Approach the presentation of these attributes with humility, acknowledging that these strengths are the result of collective efforts, continuous learning, and a steadfast commitment to improvement. Share stories and examples that highlight how these differentiators have led to successful outcomes and satisfied clients. This approach not only enhances your credibility but fosters a deeper connection with your negotiation partner, as they see the genuine value you bring to the table. Ultimately, you are not just selling a product or service; you are offering a partnership grounded in trust, integrity, and a shared vision for success. This holistic perspective ensures your negotiations are not just transactions but the beginning of enduring and mutually beneficial relationships.

Notes

_____

_____

_____

_____

_____

_____

_____

_____

_____

_____

_____

_____

_____

_____

_____

_____

_____

_____

_____

_____

_____

_____

_____

_____

_____

_____

_____

_____

_____

_____

THE SINGLE
AND MOST
DANGEROUS WORD
TO BE SPOKEN
IN BUSINESS
IS "NO."

— A. J. Darkholme

STRATEGY 6

DEVELOP A HEALTHY, ADAPTABLE MINDSET

IMAGINE YOUR NEXT negotiation starts in a few days. You've spent hours, days, weeks, maybe even months, planning and preparing. Now, it's almost game time. In this chapter, we're going to explore the important mindset preparation you'll want to do before the negotiation starts. First of all, be willing to contribute more to the negotiation process than you expect to receive. This might seem counterintuitive, but it's not. I call this the "True Give." Whatever you want to call it, this type of abundance thinking is a strong foundation for any negotiation. Don't enter a negotiation only thinking about what you want out of the deal. Remember, the best negotiations are not win or lose; they are collaborative acts of value creation that can lead to long-term partnerships with powerful benefits for everyone involved. Embrace an abundance mindset and be willing to offer true value. Give generously of your knowledge, connections, time, experience, energy, and so forth. It builds trust and respect and encourages positive behavior from your negotiating partners.

There are also some negotiation tools that can impact the tone of a negotiation— anchoring and concessions. Anchoring involves setting the initial reference point for the negotiation. Concessions open pathways to mutual agreement, and strategic compromise fosters trust and long-term relationships. You'll want to keep them in your back pocket, ready to pull out as needed. Note that the first requires planning and preparation, while the latter requires adaptability, one of the multiple intelligences that will come into play during any negotiation. By honing your knowledge and application of these tools, you're not only enhancing your effectiveness as a negotiator but you're also demonstrating your commitment to achieving fair, respectful, and successful outcomes. With these tools and a healthy, adaptable mindset, you'll build stronger, more collaborative partnerships, paving the way for sustained success and growth.

Early in *The Negotiation Code*, we talked about the self-awareness work you need to do to strengthen your negotiating skills. Part of that work is having a frank conversation with yourself around your potential biases. Maybe you're not a fan of the other team's lead negotiator. Maybe you have problems with compromise. Maybe you're fearful about the future so you want to play it safe. Maybe you don't believe you have the skills to close the deal, or you feel like you're a "bad" negotiator. These are all biases—emotional baggage that you carry into a negotiation unless you make an intentional decision to leave it at the door. The more biases you have, the heavier the baggage and the more it will weigh down the negotiation. You might need to stare your biases straight in the eye and say, "You're not joining me for this negotiation," and then confidently walk into the boardroom sans luggage. If you don't, I assure you that when negotiations get tough, that baggage will drag you down. Don't let it!

Mind Your Biases

Even the most seasoned negotiators succumb to their own biases. Maybe they are going through a rough patch, are not getting enough sleep, or are exhausted by stress. Whatever the reason, succumbing to biases is a negotiation wrecker. That's why you need to learn how to take control of your biases no matter the circumstances. If you can recognize your biases and limit their hold, you can significantly elevate your negotiating skills. This means remaining humble and committed to ongoing improvement. Of course, you're not the only negotiator trying to juggle their biases. The people across the table are challenged by their biases too. Understanding this reality is the crucial first step toward effectively mitigating the impact of biases on the health of a negotiation. Being aware of your biases will allow you to anticipate and address potential pitfalls, ensuring the negotiation remains focused on mutually beneficial outcomes. Embrace the process of identifying and mitigating biases as an opportunity for growth and learning, enhancing your ability to engage in more thoughtful and equitable negotiations. By demonstrating self-awareness and consideration, you build trust and respect with the other party. The list of biases below is long, but don't get overwhelmed. It's likely you only battle a few of these biases. But your colleagues and negotiating partners are likely battling their own set of biases, so studying this list in full will enable you to understand what they are struggling to minimize.

Confirmation Bias: The inclination to search for, interpret, and favor information that confirms one's preexisting beliefs or values. This can influence perceptions and includes the tendency to validate your initial offers and overlook counterarguments. Confirmation bias can also limit options. This type of tunnel vision may restrict the scope of your negotiations, reducing shared success possibilities.

Overconfidence Bias: The overestimation of one's abilities, knowledge, or control over a situation. This can lead to skewed judgment. You may underestimate the other party, which negatively affects your strategic planning. Overconfidence bias increases the risk of deadlock. Overconfidence can lead to unrealistic proposals, reducing the chance of agreement.

Anchoring Bias: The tendency to rely too heavily on the first piece of information encountered when making decisions. The first offer often sets the tone and range for the entire negotiation. Being the first to anchor can be advantageous, but it also poses risks if the anchor is too extreme. We'll explore anchoring in more detail shortly.

Sunk Cost Fallacy: The tendency to follow through on an endeavor if one has already invested time, effort, or money into it. This can lead to misguided persistence: You may stick with a negotiation longer than beneficial, attempting to recoup sunk costs. Sunk cost fallacy can reduce access to opportunities. Staying in a bad deal might mean missing out on better alternatives.

Zero-Sum Bias: The belief that gains for one party automatically entail losses for the other. This can reduce collaboration. Your willingness to pursue mutual gains might be limited. With a narrowed focus, you might overlook creative solutions that could enlarge the value pie for all involved.

Loss Aversion: The psychological inclination to perceive losses as more painful than gains are pleasurable. Loss aversion implies risk aversion. The fear of losses can make you overly cautious, limiting opportunities for advantageous agreements. This can lead to biased decision-making. This may result in choosing safer options that yield lesser benefits. As discussed previously, it may also create a sense of FOMO, which could prompt you to act when you otherwise wouldn't.

Groupthink: The tendency within a group to seek consensus over critical reasoning, often suppressing dissenting viewpoints. Team negotiations may suffer if members suppress alternative viewpoints for harmony. Better solutions may be overlooked in the quest for agreement.

Self-Serving Bias: The tendency to attribute successes to oneself and failures to external factors. This reduces accountability, making you less likely to admit mistakes, which affects your adaptability. When you are self-serving, it can compromise relationship building. Relations with the other party can be strained if you don't take responsibility for setbacks.

Reciprocity Bias: The psychological urge to return favors or concessions made by the other party. Reciprocity bias can lead to unplanned concessions. You might be led to give more than planned, just to reciprocate. This bias can be harnessed by the other party to make moves that benefit only them.

Availability Bias: The tendency to overvalue information that is easily recalled or at hand. Availability bias can skew your perspective. You might base decisions on recent, well-known, or emotional events rather than on a comprehensive view of the deal. The validity of your proposals, offers, and counteroffers can be adversely affected.

The Endowment Effect: The inclination to overvalue something simply because you own it. The endowment effect can lead to overvaluation. You may place unrealistically high values on your product, service, or offers, leading to an impasse. This presents a strategic risk. Negotiations could be complicated if you limit the range of acceptable outcomes.

Status Quo Bias: The preference for keeping things as they are, thereby resisting change. It promotes resistance to innovation, as you may avoid new solutions that could actually benefit all parties. Comfort impedes progress. This can hinder the development of the negotiation toward a fruitful conclusion.

The Halo Effect: The tendency to perceive someone as generally good due to one positive trait. This can lead to an overestimation of benefits. You may give too much credit to the other party's offers based on one strong point. It can create an unfavorable shift in negotiation dynamics because you may become less vigilant about other aspects of the deal.

Negativity Bias: The tendency to focus more on negative events than positive ones. Negativity bias can lead to an overabundance of cautiousness. You might focus excessively on the downsides, missing the upsides. It can create analysis paralysis. This could make you hesitant to make beneficial moves.

The Illusion of Control: The tendency to overestimate one's ability to control events. If you have an illusion of control, you may overreach. You may assume you can dictate terms more than you actually can. You could be misled into taking actions that aren't in your best interest. Remember, people don't like feeling controlled, so this could also influence the other party.

Reactance: The urge to do the opposite of what someone is trying to get you to do, to prove your autonomy. Reactance can lead to conflict escalation. Pushing too hard could lead the other party to dig in their heels. This could cause a negotiation breakdown, and it could scuttle the entire process by instigating resistance.

The Bandwagon Effect: The tendency to align our beliefs and behaviors with those of a group or trend. When the bandwagon effect comes into play, you may be subject to undue peer influence. You might feel compelled to agree with a popular opinion or trend, even if it's not in your best interest. This decreases decision integrity, and it can compromise your ability to make decisions based on your own analysis and understanding.

The Dunning-Kruger Effect: The phenomenon in which people with low competence in a domain overestimate their ability. You miscalculate your skills. You may believe you understand the situation better than you actually do. This could lead to overestimating the strength of your position or offers.

False Consensus Effect: The tendency to overestimate how much others share our beliefs and values. You make assumption errors. You may incorrectly predict the other party's responses, leading to miscalculated strategies. Your overconfidence can result in underpreparing or not seeking external input when needed.

Outcome Bias: The inclination to judge a decision based on its outcome, rather than the quality of the decision itself. This skews your judgment. Good outcomes from risky decisions may reinforce similar risky behavior in the future. This impedes your ability to learn. You may miss opportunities to learn from the decision-making process if you only focus on the end result.

The Spotlight Effect: The belief that others are observing us more closely than they actually are. This may cause you to be overcautious when you are asked to take a stance. You might be overly wary about each move due to the belief that it's under intense scrutiny. This could lead to missed opportunities. Overthinking minor details can divert attention from the larger negotiation goals.

Every human has at least one of these biases. Many of us carry around several—and most of us carry many. Don't beat yourself up. Just assess your biases and do the work. The more self-aware you become, the less your biases will control your thoughts, emotions, and behaviors. Say bye-bye to your biases before you enter a negotiation. During the negotiation, take note when you feel your biases creeping into the conversation. Keep an eye out and address the situation if others in the room fall prey to their biases. Because you're reading *The Negotiation Code*, you're developing the tools, practices, and mindset you need to redirect everyone away from their biases and back to a more productive conversation.

Anchoring in Negotiation

After you've said goodbye to your biases, it's time to throw out the anchor. Anchoring refers to setting the initial reference point or starting place for a negotiation. If the negotiation is about selling a product or service, you might start high with the idea that you'll be negotiated down. Whatever anchor you throw into the negotiation, it should be closely aligned with your goals. The anchor is also often the first offer placed on the table. As such, it holds significant weight and sets the tone for the negotiation. Anchoring is a powerful psychological concept where the first piece of information offered serves as a reference point and heavily influences the subsequent discussions and outcomes. Anchor only after careful planning and consideration. Understand that this initial proposal is not just a starting point but a powerful tool that can guide the direction of the entire negotiation. Present an offer that reflects a thoughtful balance of your interests as well as a strong understanding of the other party's needs. By doing so, you demonstrate your commitment to a fair and constructive negotiation and foster an environment of trust and collaboration. Be mindful of the implications of this first offer, using it as an opportunity to establish a positive and productive tone that paves the way for mutually beneficial outcomes. Embrace the responsibility of this pivotal moment, recognizing your approach can set the foundation for a successful and harmonious agreement that honors the goals and aspirations of both parties involved.

Through this strategic use of anchoring, you position yourself as a thoughtful and effective negotiator, dedicated to achieving excellence and building lasting, respectful relationships. Imagine, for example, you are negotiating the purchase of a large order of manufacturing equipment your company needs. To strategically influence the negotiation, you might anchor the negotiation by setting an initial price a bit lower than what you are actually willing to pay. This approach helps to steer the discussion toward a more favorable outcome, providing a reference point that can shape the entire negotiation process. By thoughtfully setting an anchor, you guide the conversation in a way that aligns with your objectives, demonstrating your preparedness and strategic insight. The key is to use anchoring as a tool to facilitate dialogue and collaboration, not as a means to dominate or undermine the other party. Through this approach, you can foster an environment of respect and cooperation, paving the way for a successful negotiation that meets the needs of all involved. By skillfully anchoring your position, you can find balanced and positive outcomes while maintaining the integrity of the negotiation process. Anchoring goes beyond just numbers like price. It encompasses factors such as your tone, the level of vulnerability you reveal, your transparency, and how much you demonstrate care for the other party, among other things.

Prepare for Concessions

Even before you throw out your anchor, you should know what adjustments and concessions you are prepared to make during a negotiation. Hopefully, this was part of your strategic planning and preparation, as recommended earlier in the book. Concessions reflect your willingness to find common ground and move closer to a mutually beneficial agreement, so prepare them with care and foresight. Concessions should never be made haphazardly. Just like objectives, concessions should align with your overall goals and strengthen your negotiating position. By thoughtfully planning your concessions, you can keep constructive conversations going, even when there's a sticking point. How? You've anticipated these sticking points and know what you're prepared to concede to keep the negotiation moving forward. This approach not only enhances your ability to reach an agreement, it also reflects your flexibility and integrity. By preparing for strategic concessions, you've positioned yourself as an effective negotiator, dedicated to creating lasting, positive relationships that benefit all parties involved.

Compromise Versus Concessions

Compromise is the delicate art of finding middle ground where both parties make concessions to reach a mutually acceptable solution. The way you frame these concessions is crucial. Rather than presenting them as sacrifices, position them as investments in both the deal and the relationship. For example, instead of saying, "We're willing to give . . ." tell your negotiating partner, "We're going to invest in . . ." This approach requires thoughtful consideration and strategic planning to ensure a mutually beneficial outcome. While compromise can foster cooperation and resolve conflicts, it is essential to approach it thoughtfully, as it can sometimes lead to lose-lose outcomes if not handled with care. By being mindful of the potential pitfalls and striving to find balanced solutions, you can turn compromise into a powerful tool for building trust and achieving lasting agreements. If both parties are willing to make reasonable adjustments without sacrificing their core interests, compromise can pave the way for innovative solutions and stronger relationships. This becomes especially important when negotiations are ongoing as part of a multiyear project. For example, suppose you are in the midst of a negotiation to expand a healthcare facility. In this complex and pivotal process, you might consider conceding on construction timelines to gain significant advantages in budget allocation or access to premium vendor services. Recognize that each concession is not merely about yielding ground but rather a strategic investment that brings you closer to achieving your overarching goals. By thoughtfully adjusting certain aspects, such as timelines, you demonstrate flexibility and a willingness to collaborate while strategically securing benefits that enhance the overall project.

This balanced approach ensures every give is accompanied by a take, fostering a spirit of mutual benefit and forward momentum. Through this method, you'll find creative solutions that align with both your immediate needs *and* long-term vision.

Conclusion

As I've mentioned before, negotiation is part art, part science. Becoming a skilled negotiator means learning an elevated approach to human interaction. Not only can this change your business or career for the better, it can also change your life for the better. Effective negotiation is supported by the three pillars of strategic planning, multiple intelligences, and continuous professional and personal growth. In addition to all this, there is a tool kit, a set of supporting skills, which we've started to explore in this chapter. Understanding biases, as well as anchoring and concessions, elevates your negotiation skills, and help you gain a psychological edge in any negotiation. Embrace the journey. Keep learning these critical skills and recognize that true negotiation prowess lies in grasping the human factor at the heart of every interaction. Approach each negotiation with humility and a genuine commitment to understanding the perspectives, emotions, and motivations of all parties. This ensures every negotiation is not just a transaction but a meaningful exchange that can lead to stronger relationships and new opportunities.

Notes

_____

_____

_____

_____

_____

_____

_____

_____

_____

_____

_____

_____

_____

_____

_____

_____

_____

_____

_____

_____

_____

_____

_____

_____

_____

_____

_____

_____

DIPLOMACY
IS THE ART
OF LETTING SOMEONE
ELSE HAVE YOUR WAY.

— *Sir David Frost*

STRATEGY 7

FRAME YOUR POSITION

FRAMING ISN'T JUST about what you see on the surface. In the context of negotiations, it can be a powerful tool for presenting information and shaping how it is received and interpreted. First, you throw out your anchor and set the initial reference point for the negotiation with your proposal. Then, you frame the presentation and proposal. Framing, which we've mentioned briefly so far in *The Negotiation Code*, is about so much more than how the facts are presented. It's about guiding the narrative to influence the course of the entire negotiation. Framing enables you to highlight the most compelling aspects of your proposal, address concerns effectively, and foster a negotiation environment rooted in trust and collaboration.

Framing should never be a one-size-fits-all strategy. Every negotiation is unique, with its own set of circumstances, stakeholders, and objectives. Therefore, it's crucial to customize your framing. This means understanding the other party's priorities, concerns, and decision-making processes. Learning how to do this is part of your long-term training and preparation. The more experience you have framing, the more opportunities you have to learn and improve. This is how you become a stronger negotiator.

Effective messaging and framing are not static. You should plan, test, and practice, but you should also be prepared to adjust and evolve as a negotiation progresses. Pay attention to how your counterpart reacts to your initial framing. Are they engaged? Do they ask follow-up questions? If not, it may be time to refine your message. Use techniques like asking for feedback or rephrasing your points to better resonate with their perspective.

Know Your Audience

One of the most critical aspects of effective framing is knowing your audience—again, this should be part of all pre-negotiation due diligence. To frame your proposals effectively, you must understand your negotiating partner's priorities, values, and concerns. This involves thorough research before the negotiation and asking insightful questions and actively listening during discussions. The earlier you know these things, the stronger the hand you'll be able to play during the negotiation. For instance, if you're negotiating with a health-care organization, their primary concern might be patient outcomes and regulatory compliance. In this case, framing your proposal around how it will improve patient care and meet compliance standards would be more compelling than focusing solely on cost savings. Or, if you're negotiating with a company that values innovation, you might frame your proposal by emphasizing how it aligns with their vision of being a market leader with cutting-edge technology. Alternatively, if you're dealing with a company that prioritizes cost savings, you might frame your proposal by highlighting the financial benefits and efficiency gains. Effectively framing your proposal so it resonates with the members of the other party—with all their specific needs and concerns—allows you to create a more persuasive and impactful narrative. This approach not only increases the likelihood of a successful outcome but also demonstrates your respect for the other party's values and priorities, fostering a more collaborative and productive negotiating environment.

Another example of strong framing was the famous Apple negotiations with music labels for iTunes. Steve Jobs didn't just present iTunes as a new platform for music sales; he framed the conversation around fighting piracy and creating a new revenue stream for the music industry—both crucial topics at the time for music labels. This strategic presentation was pivotal in gaining the support of record labels, illustrating how powerful framing can lead to significant outcomes. By understanding and applying the principles of framing, you can present your proposals in ways that resonate deeply with the other party, ensuring the conversation moves toward a mutually beneficial outcome.

This chapter will delve into various framing techniques, equipping you to enrich negotiations with greater insight, awareness, and strategic finesse. This tailored approach not only enhances your credibility but increases the likelihood of reaching a successful agreement. By framing your proposals in a way that aligns with the other party's values and objectives, you demonstrate your commitment to finding solutions that are genuinely beneficial for all involved. This positions you as a sharp negotiator, dedicated to excellence and the creation of lasting, positive value.

Flip the Frame

If you find that a negotiation is stalled or not progressing as hoped, it may be time to reframe the situation—or flip the frame. This involves shifting the focus of the negotiation to explore new angles or perspectives that may have been overlooked. This technique can be particularly useful when you encounter resistance or when the other party seems fixated on a particular issue. For example, if the other party is focused on the risks associated with a proposal, you might flip the frame by redirecting the conversation toward the potential benefits and opportunities. Alternatively, if cost is a major sticking point, you could reframe the discussion to focus on the long-term value and return on investment rather than the initial expense.

There are two types of framing: positive framing, where you highlight the benefits of an idea or proposal, and negative or loss framing, where you spotlight what could go wrong or might be lost if an idea or proposal isn't accepted. Both positive and negative framing play an important role in negotiation, and flipping the frame is the act of moving between the two types of framing. Flipping the frame requires intuition, creativity, and flexibility. It means that you are continuously reading the room, looking at issues from different angles, and being open to exploring alternative solutions. It's when all your planning, preparation, and people skills come into play—SQ, EQ, and especially AQ (adaptability). You might plan to negotiate with positive framing, but when the negotiations get tough, you might need to flip to negative framing. Understanding how to do this mid-negotiation takes strong people skills to ensure you remain authentic. That's why you should always be practicing active listening and honing your multiple intelligences. You never know when you're going to need these skills—and that's when disciplined practice pays off. If you're in top form and can redirect a stalling negotiation by flipping the frame and introducing new perspectives, you can break through impasses and drive a negotiation toward a more favorable outcome. That's intelligent negotiation—and it's an invaluable skill to have.

The way you present a proposal can drastically influence a negotiation's outcome. For instance, if you're negotiating a deal to implement new software, you might frame your proposal by highlighting how this software will increase efficiency, reduce costs, and streamline operations. By focusing on the positive impacts, you can create a compelling narrative that aligns with the other party's goals and aspirations. Conversely, negative framing in this case might focus on the risks of continuing with outdated systems, such as increased operational costs, inefficiencies, and potential security vulnerabilities. This approach can create a sense of urgency and emphasize the need for change. Negative framing leverages the psychological principle that people are generally more motivated to avoid losses than to achieve gains. For example, if you're negotiating a partnership deal, you might emphasize how the other party stands to lose market share, competitive edge, or key opportunities if they don't move forward with your proposal. This tactic is not about instilling fear but about providing a realistic assessment of the risks of inaction. When used thoughtfully, loss framing can compel the other party to make decisions more quickly. However, it's important to balance this approach with respect and consideration for the other party's perspective to ensure the conversation remains collaborative and constructive.

Both positive and negative framing have their place in negotiations. The key is to understand when and how to use each approach to guide the conversation toward the best possible outcome. By learning both types of framing, as well as developing the ability to flip between them, you can present a well-rounded case that addresses both the aspirations and concerns of the other party. This paves the way for a balanced and mutually beneficial agreement. A good example of how both types of framing and frame flipping might come into play in a single negotiation is when it's time to renew an important employee's contract. If you've heard this employee is thinking of leaving, you might start with positive framing to emphasize the benefits of staying with the company, such as continued career development and access to new opportunities. But if that doesn't make the person want to stay, you could flip the frame and try loss framing. Highlighting the significant impact of losing them might be more persuasive. Explaining how their departure could affect team morale, disrupt ongoing projects, and lead to missed opportunities for innovation and growth might be the most effective route to secure their loyalty. By illustrating the collective loss and potential setbacks that could arise, you underscore their value as a vital contributor, which makes a compelling case for their continued engagement with the company. It's essential to ensure that this isn't framed as a guilt trip but rather as a sincere expression of their value to the team and the company. With this approach, you can create a balanced and persuasive case for retention that addresses both the employee's aspirations and concerns.

Craft a Clear, Simple Message

Effective messaging shapes how your proposal is perceived. It is the narrative you construct to deliver your key points, while positioning is the strategic placement of that messaging to highlight your value and relevance. When done well, these elements guide the other party to view your proposal through a lens that resonates deeply, increasing its persuasiveness and impact. The first step is crafting your proposal for clarity. A muddled message can confuse and disengage the other party, while a clear, concise narrative builds trust and credibility. Identify the core values of your proposal—what sets it apart and makes it indispensable. Then, communicate these values in a way that speaks directly to the other party's needs and aspirations. For example, if you're negotiating a deal for sustainable packaging with an environmentally focused company, emphasize how your solution aligns with their mission to reduce waste and promote eco-friendly practices.

It's tempting to overload your messaging with details and data. However, simplicity often wins. A clear, memorable message sticks in the other party's mind and makes your proposal easier to advocate for internally. Think of Apple's iconic messaging: it's never about the technical specifications but about how the product can enhance the customer's life. Similarly, in negotiations, position your proposal in terms of the benefits it delivers, not just the features it includes.

Tailor Your Message

Just as effective framing requires you to know your audience, so does messaging. Your message should not only reflect your objectives but speak to the other party's specific concerns and priorities. Avoid generic or one-size-fits-all statements. Instead, craft messages that demonstrate your understanding of their unique situation. For instance, if you're negotiating with a risk-averse party, position your proposal as a safe, low-risk option with proven results. Conversely, if your counterpart is ambitious and growth-oriented, highlight how your proposal can help them achieve market dominance or innovation milestones.

Create Emotional Resonance with Storytelling

Negotiations are as much about emotion as logic and data. People are more likely to engage with a proposal that makes them feel understood, valued, and inspired. Use messaging to tap into your negotiating partner's emotions by highlighting shared values or the greater impact of your proposal. For example, if you're pitching a partnership to improve healthcare outcomes, you might say, "Together, we have the opportunity to revolutionize patient care and save countless lives. Let's create a legacy of health and hope." This type of messaging creates emotional resonance.

Storytelling is a powerful form of messaging that engages both the logical and emotional aspects of decision-making. A compelling story is memorable and impactful. It persuades and inspires. For example, instead of simply stating that your proposal will increase efficiency by 20 percent, you could tell the story of a customer who overcame significant challenges and saw a 20 percent improvement in efficiency. You are illustrating the same benefit, but in a deeper, more relatable way.

Stories can be positively or negatively framed—or they can be a mix. If your negotiation is being positively framed as a collaborative journey toward a shared goal, you might use stories from history about collaborations that enabled two parties to create something meaningful together. For example, in 1837, a British candlemaker named William Procter collaborated with an Irish soap maker named James Gamble to form the manufacturing company Procter & Gamble (P&G). The company's first few hit products were Ivory soap, Crisco shortening, and Tide detergent. By combining their skills and resources, P&G was able to offer a wider range of products without competing against each other. The collaboration paid off and P&G is the world's largest consumer-goods company. Alternatively, if you are negatively framing the need for collaboration, you could share a story from history about how two groups worked together to overcome or avoid a big challenge. The story of how the Allied forces worked together to defeat Hitler and the Nazis during World War II is a perfect example of a story that supports this negative framing, and one that creates strong emotional resonance as well.

Preparing stories that showcase the benefits of your proposal as well as your passion, dedication, and vision not only differentiates but makes you and your proposal more memorable and persuasive. We are wired as humans to learn through stories. They make us more receptive to people's ideas and messages. By using well-framed storytelling to your advantage, you can elevate your negotiation strategy.

Conclusion

As I mentioned at the beginning of this chapter, effective messaging, framing, and storytelling are immensely powerful negotiation tools—but they are not static. They should be tested and evolve as a negotiation progresses. These tools have the power to transform the dynamics of any negotiation by evoking emotional resonance, which are much more engaging than facts and figures. As a result, these tools can lead to more successful and impactful results. Whether you are emphasizing the benefits of a proposal, creating urgency through loss framing, flipping the frame mid-negotiation, messaging with emotion, or crafting a compelling narrative through storytelling, your ability to frame a negotiation will greatly influence its outcomes. By using framing thoughtfully and strategically, you can ensure every negotiation is not just a transaction but a meaningful exchange that honors the perspectives, emotions, and motivations of all participants.

Notes

_____

_____

_____

_____

_____

_____

_____

_____

_____

_____

_____

_____

_____

_____

_____

_____

_____

_____

_____

_____

_____

_____

_____

_____

_____

_____

_____

_____

_____

_____

_____

_____

_____

YOU CAN HAVE
EVERYTHING IN LIFE
YOU WANT, IF YOU
WILL JUST HELP
ENOUGH OTHER
PEOPLE GET WHAT
THEY WANT.

— *Zig Ziglar*

CALCULATE YOUR BEST SECONDARY OPTION (BSO™)

EVERY NEGOTIATOR NEEDS a backup plan. I call this the Best Secondary Option (BSO™). When the primary negotiation does not appear to be reaching the desired outcome, your BSO becomes a lifeline—an essential fallback strategy that ensures you are never left without a viable path forward. Defining your BSO early and clearly is critical because it offers both leverage and peace of mind. This allows you to negotiate from a position of strength and confidence. You'll adapt your BSO, but the more well-thought-out your BSO is in advance, the more significantly it can influence the dynamics of your negotiation. For example, imagine you are negotiating a crucial partnership deal. If the terms are not aligning with your strategic goals, having a BSO—such as an alternative partner or a different strategic initiative—empowers you to walk away without fear of losing ground. This knowledge enables you to push for the best possible terms while remaining calm and composed because you know you have a viable plan ready if the negotiation doesn't go your way. Embracing the BSO as a critical element of your negotiation tool kit demonstrates not only your preparedness but your resilience. It shows you are not only focused on the current deal but are thinking several steps ahead, ready to adapt to changing circumstances. By having a robust secondary option, you demonstrate you understand that not all negotiations will result in the desired outcome, and you're ready to pivot, if need be. This strategic approach not only enhances your negotiation skills but increases your chances for a successful outcome.

Crafting a strong BSO gives you an invaluable psychological advantage, allowing you to negotiate in a calm and composed manner, even when the conversation gets tough. For example, if you are in discussions to secure a new client contract, knowing your BSO—such as having alternative clients or projects lined up—ensures you can negotiate assertively and without desperation. This mental assurance not only enhances your negotiation effectiveness but also demonstrates your unwavering commitment to achieving the best possible results while maintaining your integrity and peace of mind. By being clear on your BSO, you transform potential anxiety into a source of strength, fostering a sense of security and empowerment that drives you toward success with grace and confidence.

Determine Your BSO

The first step in leveraging your BSO is to clearly identify it. What is your best option should a negotiation hit a wall or even collapse? It's not enough to have a vague idea; you must meticulously define and quantify your fallback options. Your BSO represents specific alternatives as well as the least acceptable outcome—that is, the baseline agreement below which you will not go. This distinction is crucial because it separates your ideal goals and acceptable concessions from the minimum you're willing to accept. It is your reserve point. Unlike optimal outcomes, where you reach for the stars, a BSO is your safety net. For example, if you are negotiating a supplier contract, your BSO might be working with a different supplier who charges slightly more but also offers more reliable service. By selecting this alternative, you ensure you have an option if your current supplier doesn't rise to the occasion and meet your needs. Having the second supplier in your back pocket reinforces your position and enables you to negotiate without fear. You demonstrate to your negotiating partner that you're strategic and have planned for surprises.

Commit to Continuous BSO Improvement

Continuously seeking opportunities to enhance your BSO is vital for maintaining a strong negotiating position. Think of your BSO in dynamic terms. You have an initial BSO, but you're ready to improve it as opportunities present themselves during the negotiation. This is important because the more robust and viable your BSO, the greater your leverage at the negotiating table. Reassess your BSO as new information becomes available throughout the course of negotiations. Staying informed and flexible is key. Each piece of new information offers an opportunity to refine and enhance your BSO, ensuring it remains a strong alternative should the primary negotiation not yield your desired outcome. For example, if you discover additional potential partners or alternative solutions during negotiations, incorporate these insights into your BSO to strengthen your fallback plan.

Understand the Other Party's BSO

Just as you carefully assess your own BSO, it is equally important to strive to understand the BSO of the other party. This
knowledge can be a powerful tool in negotiations, offering
deeper insights into their position and potential vulnerabilities. Approach this with humility and a genuine interest in
creating a balanced and mutually beneficial agreement. By
comprehending the other party's fallback plan, you can strategically enhance your negotiating position. For instance, if
you recognize that their alternative options are less favorable
or more limited than yours, you can confidently propose terms
that align with your goals while still offering value to them.
This thoughtful and empathetic approach not only strengthens your negotiating leverage but also fosters an environment of trust and respect. It demonstrates your commitment
to understanding the full scope of the negotiation landscape,
ensuring you are well-prepared to find solutions that benefit
both parties. Ultimately, by gaining insight into the other party's BSO, you position yourself as a strategic, considerate, and
effective negotiator dedicated to achieving excellence and fostering long-term, positive relationships. Here are some steps
you can take to determine the other party's BSO:

1. **Ask Strategic Questions:** Craft a set of questions
   that will help illuminate and clarify each negotiating party's BSO. This proactive approach deepens
   your understanding of the negotiation landscape
   and fosters an environment of transparency and
   collaboration. For instance, you might ask questions like, "What alternative solutions would you
   consider if this agreement doesn't materialize?" or

"What are the key priorities that must be met for you to consider other options?" By asking these insightful questions, you can guide the conversation toward uncovering critical information that helps both sides better understand their positions and constraints. This strategic questioning strengthens your negotiating position and demonstrates your commitment to understanding and addressing the needs and concerns of all parties involved. You might be amazed at how much people are willing to share when you take the time to simply ask.

2. **Rate Answers for Strength:** Once you have answers to your strategic questions about the other party's BSO, it's time to rate them for strength. The number one represents the answers that indicate the other party has a weak BSO, while ten represents answers that indicate they have a strong BSO. This exercise is the first step in assessing how well you understand the other party's position. Recognize that striving for greater clarity not only strengthens your negotiating position but also enhances the overall effectiveness and fairness of the negotiation process. That's why it's worth your time and attention.

3. **Calculate the Average:** Once you have rated each question for perceived strength, sum up all the individual ratings and then divide this number by the total number of questions you've asked. This calculation provides you with a perceived strength score, offering valuable insight into your overall

understanding of each negotiating party's BSO. The higher this score, the stronger their BSO. This process is not just about achieving a numerical value but about enhancing your strategic preparedness and effectiveness as a negotiator. By reflecting on your scores, you can identify areas where new questions and deeper inquiry are needed. By diligently rating and revising your questions in search of more clarity, you show dedication to understanding all positions. This sharpens your insights and ultimately empowers you to engage in negotiations with more confidence.

4. **Interpret Scores:** Achieving a score of seven or above indicates a strong BSO. It reflects a high level of clarity and preparedness. As a negotiator, a high score means you have a clear understanding of the other party's BSO, even though you don't have all the information yet. Conversely, a score of three or below suggests the BSO is weak and requires further work. If you have a low score, it's an opportunity to learn and grow. Understand that these scores are not just numbers but valuable indicators of where you stand and where you need to improve. The goal is to be well-equipped to navigate and adapt strategically during negotiations based on the information you have. By striving to achieve a stronger understanding of the other party's BSO, you demonstrate your commitment to achieving the best possible outcomes. Keep in mind that your goal should always be ambitious and informed by the strength of the other party's BSO. This is completely independent of your own

BSO, which forms the basis of your reserve point. These two factors are entirely separate and should not influence each other.

THE ULTIMATE GOAL ALIGNMENT GRID

THEIR BSO (Defines Your Goal)	YOUR BSO (Defines Your Reservation Point)
↓	↓
Your Ambitious Goal	Your Minimum Acceptable Outcome (Reservation)
↑	↑
Weak BSO (Theirs) (Opportunity for ambitious goals)	Strong BSO (Yours) (Higher minimum reservation)

Keep Your BSO Secret

Guard your BSO with care. Revealing it too early—or sometimes revealing it at all—in the negotiation process can inadvertently weaken your position. Maintaining a level of discretion about your BSO allows you to negotiate from a place of strength. You retain the advantage of flexibility, ensuring you can respond to the dynamics of the negotiation without prematurely limiting your options. If you disclose your BSO too soon, the other party may leverage this information to their advantage, potentially undermining your ability to secure the best possible terms. Your BSO should be your silent source of strength, empowering you to negotiate assertively and strategically. By holding your BSO close, you position yourself as an astute negotiator.

Practice BSO Scenarios

I encourage negotiators to practice scenarios that might happen during their negotiations so they can be prepared to revise their BSOs accordingly. Every negotiation is different, but here are a few scenarios to help you understand what I mean. Let's start with a mergers and acquisitions scenario. Imagine you are leading an acquisition deal for your company. In this scenario, your BSO might involve partnering with another company instead of proceeding with the acquisition. For instance, consider the case of a tech firm looking to acquire a smaller startup to gain access to innovative technology. If the acquisition negotiations become challenging or the terms are not aligning with your strategic objectives, having a well-defined BSO—such as forming a strategic alliance with another firm that offers similar technological advancements—provides you with a powerful alternative. Knowing you have this viable option in your back pocket allows you to maintain composure throughout the negotiation, free of fear that you might lose out if the acquisition does not move forward. This enables you to stay clear minded and focused on achieving the best possible outcome for your company. By practicing scenarios with your BSO, you demonstrate strategic foresight and resilience, showcasing your commitment to achieving your goals through multiple pathways.

On a more personal note, if the scenario is about you throwing your hat in the ring for an exciting new role, a BSO can help. Have another job offer already in hand as your BSO. Knowing you have this alternative opportunity empowers you to approach the salary and benefits package negotiations with greater confidence and clarity. This awareness allows you to articulate your value and negotiate assertively, secure in the knowledge that you have a strong fallback option. Having a BSO allows you to approach every negotiation with greater confidence and resolve.

Conclusion

Your BSO serves as both a safety net and a compass, guiding you through the intricacies of a negotiation. It provides you with clarity and confidence because you know precisely when to walk away or when to press on for a better deal. Recognize that your BSO not only protects you but supports your position. And by gaining insight into the other party's BSO, you can sharpen your own BSO. This approach needs to be the cornerstone of your negotiation strategy because it ensures you are always prepared to push hard to attain optimal outcomes but are also capable of resilience if things don't land the way you want. Either way, a BSO empowers you to achieve the best possible outcomes.

Notes

_____

_____

_____

_____

_____

_____

_____

_____

_____

_____

_____

_____

_____

_____

_____

EMOTIONS ARE
AS CRITICAL
AS LOGIC IN ANY
NEGOTIATION.

— *Wendy Sherman*

STRATEGY 9

CREATE YOUR NEGOTIATING GRID™

THE NEGOTIATING GRID™ is your playbook—a meticulously crafted matrix with which you categorize various options, alternatives, and desired outcomes. This grid serves as a strategic road map, guiding you through the complex maze of negotiations with confidence and precision. The grid enables you to pull all the actions outlined in this book into a single framework. By using the Negotiating Grid, you can systematically visualize the entire landscape of possibilities, helping you identify the most advantageous paths to achieve your desired outcomes in a negotiation. This framework allows you to organize your thoughts and strategies in a way that enables you to anticipate challenges, prepare responses, and create contingency plans that enhance your adaptability and resilience. Approach the Negotiating Grid with a genuine desire to achieve mutually beneficial results for all parties. Recognize that the best negotiations are those during which everyone feels valued, respected, and understood. When used correctly, the Negotiating Grid helps you foster collaboration, build trust, and stay aligned with your overarching goals. Embrace this tool as your guiding compass and let it illuminate the way forward and transform complex negotiations into opportunities for success and growth. By leveraging the grid's insights, you position yourself as a thoughtful, strategic, and reliable negotiating partner, dedicated to achieving excellence in every interaction.

The Negotiating Grid Format

As you prepare for your next negotiation, take the time to meticulously list all your deal points within the Negotiating Grid format. This structured approach allows you to clearly note the importance of each element while thoughtfully estimating their significance to the other party. This comprehensive matrix enables you to see the full scope of the negotiation landscape and prioritize your own objectives while remaining flexible and open to finding mutually beneficial solutions. By visualizing the interplay of various deal points, you can strategically plan your next moves and anticipate potential areas of compromise, ensuring you are well-prepared to navigate the negotiation with confidence and clarity. This not only strengthens your position but highlights your commitment to achieving a fair and balanced agreement.

Understand the Other Party's Grid

A powerful negotiator doesn't just map their own positions—they also **anticipate and analyze the other party's grid**. Understanding their priorities, constraints, and trade-offs allows you to position your proposal for maximum acceptance.

1. **Identify Their High-Priority Items**
   What are they most unwilling to compromise on?
   These are their **deal-breakers**.

2. **Pinpoint Their Low-Priority Concessions**
   What matters less to them but is valuable to you?
   These are your **leverage points**.

3. **Assess Their Best Secondary Option (BSO)**
   If they walk away, what's their best alternative?
   Position your proposal **as a superior choice** to their fallback option.

4. **Adjust Your Messaging Accordingly**
   If you know where their **pressure points** are, you can **frame your offer** as the best way to meet their objectives.

By understanding the other party's grid, you move from reacting to **strategically shaping the negotiation**, ensuring your offer aligns with their reality while still **advancing your own interests.**

Deal Points

Deal points are the core aims and negotiable elements of a proposal, encompassing aspects such as price, quantity, incentives, and more. These elements shape the overall agreement by reflecting the diverse interests and priorities of both parties. Some deal points are fixed and form the foundation of the agreement, while others are flexible and serve as opportunities for trade-offs to create mutual value. Approaching deal points with strategic intent and adaptability allows you to structure agreements that are both competitive and sustainable. Recognizing what is essential versus what is negotiable ensures you maintain control while fostering collaboration. By identifying where trade-offs can be made—such as adjusting pricing structures, offering incentives, or providing additional services—you can unlock value and strengthen the partnership.

To use deal points effectively, you'll want to start with the Fixed Deal Points, which are the essential terms both parties aim to achieve. These are established at the outset of a negotiation. Next, you want to explore Flexible Deal Points. These are the trade-offs you and your negotiating partner are willing to make. As you gain insights throughout a negotiation, you can adjust your negotiable elements to find middle ground and resolve conflicts while protecting the core deal structure.

Simplified Comparison

Aspect	Fixed Deal Points	Flexible Deal Points (Trade-Offs)
Definition	Core elements of agreement.	Negotiable aspects that create flexibility.
Purpose	Define essential structure of deal.	Enable compromise and collaboration.
Focus	Outcomes and goals of agreement.	Process of reaching alignment on goals.
Examples	Scope, financial terms, duration.	Discounts, extended payment terms.
Flexibility	Often fixed or minimally flexible.	Highly negotiable based on priorities.

Weighted Scoring of Deal Points

Assigning values to different deal points based on their importance in the negotiation is a strategic approach that helps you make informed decisions swiftly and effectively. This method allows you to prioritize your objectives and understand the relative significance of each element in the context of the overall deal. By thoughtfully evaluating and assigning weight to each deal point, you ensure your negotiation strategy is both comprehensive and focused, enabling you to respond to opportunities and challenges with agility and confidence. For instance, in a business partnership negotiation, you might assign higher values to deal points such as delivery timelines and quality standards, which are critical to maintaining operational efficiency and customer satisfaction. On the other hand, aspects like payment terms and minimum order quantities might be assigned slightly lower values, reflecting their secondary importance in a particular negotiation. By having these values clearly defined, you can quickly assess trade-offs and make decisions that align with your strategic priorities. This approach not only streamlines the negotiation process but demonstrates your preparedness and commitment to achieving a fair and successful outcome.

Utilize your Negotiating Grid to thoughtfully identify the range in which both parties can achieve a mutually beneficial agreement. This strategic approach emphasizes the importance of creating a shared success scenario, where the interests and priorities of both sides are met in a balanced and equitable manner. Begin by mapping out your objectives and those of the other party, seeking areas of overlap and alignment that can serve as the foundation for a successful agreement. This not only streamlines the negotiation process but builds trust and rapport, showing you are invested in finding solutions that work for everyone involved. For example, in a business partnership negotiation, you might find that both parties highly value innovation and market expansion. By focusing on these shared priorities, you can propose initiatives and agreements that enhance both parties' growth potential and competitive edge, instead of focusing on price. This thoughtful and strategic use of the Negotiating Grid ensures you are well-prepared to make decisions that benefit both sides, paving the way for a strong, enduring partnership.

THE NEGOTIATION GRID™

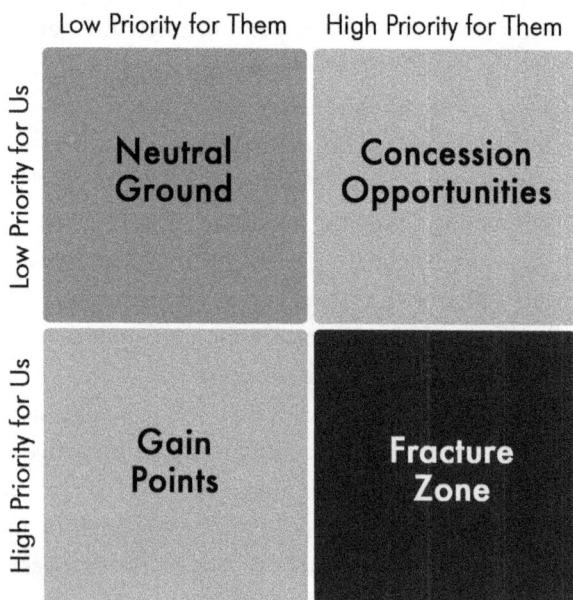

	Low Priority for Them	High Priority for Them
Low Priority for Us	Neutral Ground	Concession Opportunities
High Priority for Us	Gain Points	Fracture Zone

Here's a deeper dive into each of the elements in the chart, each made up of various deal points.

Fracture Zone: The fracture zone is where both parties have significant stakes and the potential to achieve mutually beneficial outcomes. However, this is also the area where the risk of tension, disagreement, and breakdown is the highest. It is within this zone that true collaborative success can be realized, as both sides work toward solutions that address their most important needs and objectives. But reaching agreement in this space is rarely possible without leveraging the other zones.

The items in the fracture zone often spark contention because they involve deeply held interests and priorities. These are typically areas where perspectives diverge sharply, making them challenging to navigate. Critical deal points such as price, ownership rights, exclusivity, and long-term commitments tend to fall into this category. Because of the weight these issues carry, emotions often run high, and the potential for progress can be overshadowed by the likelihood of disputes. When these issues are mishandled or approached with rigidity, they can stall negotiations or even cause them to break down entirely.

The metaphor of a "fracture" highlights the fragility of this space. Just as a fracture in a structure can lead to its collapse if left unaddressed, unresolved conflicts in this zone can threaten the entire negotiation. Missteps, ultimatums, or an unwillingness to engage strategically can cause the process to splinter. To navigate it effectively, negotiators must proceed with caution, sensitivity, and a structured approach, avoiding unnecessary pressure while focusing on de-escalation, compromise, and the integration of other deal points to balance priorities.

Price, as a key item in the fracture zone, should be the only variable within this zone across your UNO™ options. Ensure price adjustments are minimal and positioned toward the lower end of the options hierarchy in your UNO, making it less likely to become the primary focus of the negotiation. By doing so, you retain control over the discussion while preserving the integrity of your gain points and other critical elements.

Successfully managing the fracture zone requires acknowledging and accepting its contentious nature early in the process. By proactively identifying the challenges that exist in this space, you can set expectations, prepare for potential points of friction, and cultivate a more constructive dialogue. Rather than allowing disagreements to derail progress, it's important to recognize that this zone presents an opportunity to align interests in a way that strengthens the final agreement. The high stakes in this area often drive both parties to engage more earnestly, provided they approach negotiations with a commitment to understanding each other's perspective.

This is why the fracture zone cannot be addressed in isolation; it must be balanced with concessions and gain points from the other zones. By structuring negotiations to incorporate flexibility and mutual benefit, you create the conditions necessary to resolve the most difficult issues. A rigid approach in this space often leads to an impasse, while a strategic approach fosters collaboration and trust.

Approaching these discussions with humility and adaptability allows for more meaningful outcomes. Instead of focusing solely on what separates both sides, consider how the negotiation can be framed around shared objectives. Rather than seeing a contested issue as a potential deal-breaker, it should be positioned as a problem to be solved together. A well-managed fracture zone results in agreements that are not only fair but sustainable. The outcome is a balanced, equitable, and sustainable agreement—one that reflects a partnership built on respect and mutual gain. Working through this high-stakes zone with a collaborative mindset leads to stronger relationships, innovative solutions, and shared growth. A negotiator who prioritizes agreements in all areas, rather than fixating solely on points of friction, positions themselves as someone who is not focused on "winning" but on building lasting, impactful partnerships that benefit all involved.

Gain Points: Gain points are elements within a negotiation that hold significant importance for you but are of lesser concern to the other party. These points offer a strategic advantage, as they allow you to secure favorable terms with minimal resistance. Recognizing and leveraging gain points is a key aspect of effective negotiation, as it enables you to align your priorities with opportunities the other party is more willing to accommodate. By identifying and articulating these gain points, you can navigate the negotiation process with greater ease and confidence, ensuring your most critical needs are met without creating unnecessary friction. By skillfully utilizing gain points, you demonstrate your strategic acumen and commitment to achieving mutually beneficial outcomes. This, in turn, builds trust and reinforces your reputation as a fair and empathetic negotiator dedicated to fostering long-term, positive relationships that drive success for all involved.

Concession Opportunities: As discussed in earlier chapters, concessions are elements within a negotiation with which you are willing to make compromises in order to gain advantages elsewhere, ideally within the fracture zone. Concession opportunities should include items that can be adjusted or traded off without compromising your core interests. Examples include flexible timelines, service levels, exclusive terms or add-ons, extended warranties, or optional features. Begin negotiations by highlighting these intangible elements that hold perceived value for the other party. These items can offer significant perceived benefits without incurring substantial costs to you. This approach builds goodwill and creates room for collaboration before addressing more contentious issues.

Understanding and strategically utilizing concessions is a crucial part of a successful negotiation, as it involves identifying areas where you can afford to be flexible without sacrificing your core objectives. By thoughtfully offering concessions, you can create opportunities for the other party to reciprocate, fostering a collaborative and respectful negotiation environment. Emphasize the importance of these strategic concessions in facilitating progress and reaching agreements that satisfy both parties' interests. By aligning your concessions with the fracture zone, you ensure the compromises made are within the range in which both sides can find acceptable solutions. This approach not only enhances your negotiation strategy but also builds trust and rapport, as the other party recognizes your flexibility and dedication to finding equitable solutions. Ultimately, skillful management of concessions highlights your strategic acumen and reinforces your role as a fair and empathetic negotiator committed to fostering long-term, successful partnerships that benefit all involved.

Neutral Ground: When issues are of low priority for both sides, they present a valuable opportunity to be settled quickly, often serving as a catalyst for building goodwill and fostering a positive negotiation atmosphere. Recognizing these less critical points allows both parties to achieve quick wins early in the negotiation process, creating a foundation of trust and cooperation. By swiftly resolving these minor issues, you set a constructive tone for the more challenging aspects of the negotiation, showing that you are dedicated to finding common ground and advancing mutual interests. These small victories not only streamline the negotiation process but also build momentum and positive rapport, paving the way for more significant agreements. Emphasize the importance of these early resolutions as a means to establish a spirit of collaboration and respect, reinforcing the idea that both sides are working together toward a shared goal. Exclude these from your UNO but use them to foster connection and establish common ground during discussions.

Keep Your Grid Handy: Always keep your Negotiating Grid accessible during negotiations, as it serves as an invaluable blueprint. This essential tool provides a structured framework that guides you through the complexities of the negotiation process, ensuring you remain focused and well-prepared at every stage. By having the Negotiating Grid at your fingertips, you can quickly reference key deal points, prioritize your objectives, and assess potential trade-offs with confidence and clarity. This allows you to make informed decisions on the spot, enhancing your ability to respond to dynamic situations and shifting demands. Share your Negotiation Grid with your negotiation teammates, demonstrating transparency and a collaborative spirit. This approach not only reinforces your credibility but also fosters a sense of trust and respect, as it shows your dedication to a fair and structured negotiation process. Ultimately, by keeping your Negotiating Grid accessible, you position yourself as a disciplined and strategic negotiator, ready to navigate the negotiation landscape with precision and purpose, all while maintaining a focus on achieving excellence and mutual success for all parties involved.

Explore Industry Applications: The Negotiating Grid can be used for almost any industry and for many use cases. Here are some scenarios where the grid could come in handy.

Mergers and Acquisitions: Imagine acquiring a pioneering tech company that has built a niche in robotics automation. You start by employing the Negotiating Grid to identify and categorize critical deal elements. Gain points could include retaining engineering talent or acquiring access to their advanced training programs—assets that bring immense value to your goals but are not primary concerns for the seller. These elements offer opportunities to enhance your operations with minimal resistance.

However, key issues such as exclusive rights to proprietary robotics designs or control over their global distribution channels will fall squarely into the fracture zone. Both sides have substantial stakes in these high-value elements, and achieving agreement here requires a strategic blend of compromise and creativity. For example, you might propose a shared development framework that allows the seller to retain partial royalties in exchange for exclusive licensing in your core market. This balances the seller's financial interests while securing your competitive advantage.

To unlock further value, look at concession opportunities such as assuming responsibility for certain transition costs or offering incentives tied to performance milestones. These concessions can help ease tensions in the fracture zone by addressing concerns that are highly significant to the seller but less costly for your side. Don't overlook neutral ground items such as minor noncompete clauses or standard legal terms—resolving these efficiently can foster goodwill early in the process.

Through this structured approach, the grid helps you negotiate a deal that not only strengthens your strategic position but also builds a collaborative foundation for success. With every decision aligned to your long-term objectives, you secure an acquisition that enhances both companies' legacies while preparing for sustained growth.

Vendor Negotiations: Imagine you're a growing food brand negotiating with a supplier to secure premium ingredients for a new product launch. The Negotiating Grid offers a clear framework to assess key factors like cost, quality, and reliability. Gain points could include locking in priority access to fresh produce—critical for your brand's differentiation but manageable for the supplier to provide due to their surplus capacity. Leveraging these points can give you a competitive edge without significantly impacting the supplier's operations. At the same time, elements like volume discounts or guaranteed delivery schedules may land in the fracture zone. Both parties recognize the importance of these deal points, and tensions may arise as you try to align priorities. To resolve this, consider proposing a flexible purchasing agreement that adjusts order sizes based on seasonal availability, giving the supplier breathing room while ensuring you meet customer demand.

On the other hand, concession opportunities could involve extending payment terms to support the supplier's cash flow or agreeing to a multiyear contract to provide them with stability. These concessions, while beneficial to the supplier, can also strengthen your supply chain in the long term. Address neutral ground matters like packaging specifications or standard shipping terms early on to build rapport and maintain momentum. This comprehensive approach ensures you not only negotiate a fair deal but also build a strong supplier relationship that aligns with your growth trajectory. By balancing priorities and fostering collaboration, you pave the way for a partnership that delivers mutual success.

Employee Benefits Negotiation: Imagine hiring a marketing executive who could transform your brand's online presence. The Negotiating Grid becomes your tool to craft an offer that aligns with both your priorities and the candidate's expectations. Gain points might include offering leadership opportunities or funding for professional certifications—benefits that are valuable to the candidate but come at a low cost to your organization. These elements can demonstrate your commitment to their growth while addressing their career goals. However, certain aspects like equity options or performance-based bonuses may fall into the fracture zone, where both parties have strong interests. Negotiating these elements requires transparency and flexibility, such as tying equity grants to measurable performance metrics. This ensures alignment with both the candidate's aspirations and your company's strategic goals. Concession opportunities could involve offering additional vacation days or flexible remote work arrangements—perks that are highly valued by the candidate but manageable for you to provide. Resolve neutral ground issues, such as minor administrative perks, quickly to establish a positive tone. By approaching the negotiation with collaboration and empathy, you demonstrate that your organization values talent and fosters a culture of mutual respect. This thoughtful process results in a compensation package that not only attracts top talent but also positions them for long-term success within your team.

Franchise Agreements: Picture negotiating a franchise deal for a fast-growing fitness brand. The Negotiating

Grid allows you to break down factors such as territory rights, fees, and support services. Gain points might include offering access to proprietary fitness technology or regional marketing campaigns—benefits critical to the franchisee's success but manageable within your budget. Highlighting these points helps reinforce the value of joining your brand.

Critical issues, such as territory exclusivity or fee structures, will likely land in the fracture zone, where both sides have high stakes. To navigate this, propose phased exclusivity based on performance metrics or consider tiered fee structures that reduce up-front costs while ensuring long-term profitability for your brand.

Concession opportunities, such as providing extended training support or reduced initial franchise fees, can help attract franchisees who align with your vision. Address neutral ground items like standard operating procedures or branding guidelines efficiently to create a smooth negotiation process.

This balanced approach ensures the franchise agreement fosters mutual growth while maintaining consistency in brand values. By focusing on strategic priorities and fostering trust, you create a foundation for successful franchise partnerships.

Real Estate Transactions: Imagine negotiating a lease for a prime commercial property that could elevate your flagship store. The Negotiating Grid helps you prioritize factors like location, lease terms, and renovation responsibilities. Gain points might include negotiating early access for build-outs or securing on-site parking rights, which enhance your operations without imposing significant costs on the landlord. Issues like rental pricing or long-term lease options will likely fall into the fracture zone, where both sides must carefully balance competing interests. Consider structuring rent escalation clauses that tie increases to revenue performance, aligning the landlord's incentives with your success.

Leverage concession opportunities, such as offering an extended lease term or shouldering specific maintenance responsibilities, to address the landlord's concerns. Resolve neutral ground items, like signage restrictions, efficiently to establish a positive negotiation atmosphere. By addressing each element with a strategic mindset, you secure a lease agreement that supports both operational goals and financial stability, fostering a constructive landlord-tenant relationship.

Technology Partnerships: You're exploring a partnership with a software developer to integrate AI into your customer support systems. The Negotiating Grid provides clarity as you evaluate compatibility, IP ownership, and development timelines. Gain points could include prioritizing comarketing opportunities or early access to beta features—valuable to you but achievable for the developer with minimal effort.

Ownership of intellectual property, however, may land firmly in the fracture zone. Propose creative solutions, such as co-ownership with royalties, to address both parties' stakes in the innovation. This approach can mitigate risks while ensuring mutual growth.

Concession opportunities might involve adjusting delivery deadlines or offering up-front payments to address the developer's resource constraints. Resolve neutral ground issues like support level agreements quickly to maintain momentum. This process ensures the partnership drives technological advancements while strengthening both organizations.

Distribution Agreements: Imagine negotiating a distribution agreement to launch your product in international markets. Use the Negotiating Grid to prioritize factors like territory coverage, order volumes, and payment terms. Gain points might include securing dedicated shelf space or early access to distributor networks—benefits critical to your expansion strategy but easily provided by the distributor due to their existing infrastructure. However, elements such as exclusive distribution rights or guaranteed minimum orders will likely fall into the fracture zone, where both sides have significant stakes. To resolve these challenges, consider structuring an agreement with tiered minimums that grow based on performance metrics, allowing both parties to share risk and reward.

Leverage concession opportunities such as offering flexible payment terms or reduced initial pricing to incentivize the distributor's commitment to your product. Resolve neutral ground items, like standard indemnity clauses, quickly to maintain positive momentum. This comprehensive approach ensures your distribution agreement is both strategically advantageous and sustainable, fostering a partnership that drives growth and mutual success across new markets.

Regulatory Compliance: Consider navigating a healthcare partnership where regulatory compliance is a nonnegotiable requirement. Start with the Negotiating Grid to assign priority to compliance factors such as health and safety standards, reporting obligations, and certification timelines. Gain points might include leveraging advanced compliance tools or securing preferred audit schedules—valuable to your organization but simpler for the partner to implement. Critical elements such as adapting existing workflows to meet your organization's regulatory requirements are likely to fall into the fracture zone. To address this, propose a phased implementation plan that balances your need for adherence with their capacity for operational adjustments. This ensures that both parties remain aligned without overburdening the partnership.

Concession opportunities could involve assuming responsibility for additional documentation or extending training support to the partner's staff to meet compliance standards. Resolve neutral ground items, such as routine certification renewals, efficiently to establish goodwill early in the negotiation. This structured approach ensures that compliance remains a cornerstone of your partnership while creating room for mutual success and operational efficiency.

Customer Contracts: Picture negotiating a multiyear service agreement with a major corporate client. The Negotiating Grid helps you break down the deal into manageable priorities. Gain points might include locking in annual price reviews or securing advance payments for premium tiers of service—benefits that protect your bottom line without significantly impacting the client. However, key issues such as exclusivity or termination clauses are likely to fall into the fracture zone, where competing interests must be resolved thoughtfully. Propose alternatives like performance-based exclusivity or staggered termination fees that balance risks and rewards for both sides.

Leverage concession opportunities, such as offering expanded service guarantees or extending contract durations, to meet the client's priorities while securing their commitment. Resolve neutral ground items, such as minor data-sharing agreements, quickly to maintain goodwill and momentum. By structuring the negotiation around shared goals and mutual trust, you create a balanced and sustainable agreement that fosters a long-term partnership.

Investor Relations: Imagine seeking to raise capital for a transformative product line in a competitive market. Use the Negotiating Grid to evaluate factors like equity distribution, valuation benchmarks, and governance rights. Gain points might include structuring milestone-based funding rounds or securing board observer seats—terms that support your vision without materially impacting the investor's control.

High-stakes issues, such as equity ownership or voting rights, will likely fall into the fracture zone. Address these concerns by proposing innovative solutions like dual-class shares or capped voting rights, ensuring that investor interests are protected while preserving your operational autonomy. Leverage concession opportunities, such as offering enhanced reporting standards or investor exclusivity rights for future funding rounds, to sweeten the deal. Resolve neutral ground items, like standard due diligence processes, quickly to keep the focus on key priorities. This thoughtful and strategic approach ensures you secure funding while building trust with investors, creating a foundation for long-term growth and success.

Conclusion

The Negotiating Grid provides a structured and strategic approach to navigating complex, multivariable negotiations. It serves as more than just a tool for tracking various factors; it is a comprehensive framework designed to empower you to make well-informed decisions that pave the way for shared success outcomes for all parties involved. By meticulously organizing and prioritizing each variable, the Negotiating Grid helps you to clearly see the landscape of the negotiation, enabling you to anticipate challenges and identify opportunities for collaboration and mutual benefit. This approach fosters an environment of trust and respect, as it demonstrates your commitment to achieving a fair and balanced agreement that takes into account the needs and objectives of everyone at the table. Embrace the Negotiating Grid with humility and a genuine desire to find common ground, showing you are dedicated to creating solutions that are equitable and beneficial for all stakeholders. By using this thoughtful and strategic method, you can transform even the most complex negotiations into opportunities for building strong, enduring partnerships that drive collective success and long-term growth.

Notes

_____

_____

_____

_____

_____

_____

_____

_____

_____

_____

_____

_____

_____

_____

_____

CREATE YOUR NEGOTIATING GRID™

YOU NEVER GET
A SECOND CHANCE
TO MAKE A FIRST
IMPRESSION.

— *Will Rogers*

BRING EVERYTHING TOGETHER WITH THE UNO™ COMPARISON MATRIX

AS IS PROBABLY clear to you by now, negotiations are seldom about a single issue. Typically, they are complex and multifaceted. Integrating all elements of a negotiation into a unified strategy builds clarity and confidence. It incorporates your unique value proposition along with all your research and planning. By bringing everything together, you enhance the appeal of your offer or solution while showing you're cognizant of the multiple interests and needs of all parties involved in the negotiation. This comprehensive approach demonstrates your commitment to mutually beneficial solutions and thus maximizes your potential for success. This approach also allows you to see where negotiating elements interconnect, making the negotiation process more dynamic and effective. Using the Unified Negotiation Options

Comparison Matrix, or UNO Comparison Matrix for short, which is explained in detail below, you not only highlight all the benefits of your offer but also encourage the other party to reveal their key interests and needs. This strategic approach helps you tailor your negotiation tactics effectively, ensuring you address the most important aspects of the deal for both sides, setting everyone up for success.

The UNO Comparison Matrix

The organization of the UNO Comparison Matrix comes from the Negotiation Grid. The grid brings everything together in two documents—an internal one for your planning and insights, and an external one that's part of the proposal you share with the other party in the negotiation. This critical tool visually presents three comprehensive package deals, allowing the other party to see the full scope of your offering in a single document. The matrix highlights the integrated benefits of each option, showcasing how the various trade point elements work together to create a balanced and appealing offer. For maximum impact, the matrix should be presented in person whenever possible. This way, you can engage directly, addressing any concerns immediately and ensuring the nuances of your offer are fully and clearly communicated—and everyone's questions are answered in real-time. With its three side-by-side offerings, the UNO Comparison Matrix helps everyone understand the full scope of your offering. With an emphasis on clarity and simplicity, it significantly reduces the risk of confusion or misunderstanding.

Deal Points	Package 1	Package 2	Package 3
Concession Opportunities (Varies Across Packages)	Extended payment terms (high value to them, low impact on cash flow).	Discounts for up-front payment (trade-off against long-term support).	More flexible contract termination clauses (low impact for you, high value for them).
Gain Point (Held Constant Across Packages)	Inclusion of quarterly business reviews (important for relationship building).	Inclusion of quarterly business reviews (important for relationship building).	Inclusion of quarterly business reviews (important for relationship building).
Fracture Zone Item (Held Constant Across Packages)	Codevelopment of new features aligned with both parties' goals.	Codevelopment of new features aligned with both parties' goals.	Codevelopment of new features aligned with both parties' goals.
Price (Fracture Zone Item – May Vary or Be Held Constant)	Mid-tier pricing with extended payment terms.	High pricing with premium support and training.	Lower pricing with minimal extras.
Gain Point (Held Constant Across Packages)	Premium SLA with guaranteed response times (high value to them, moderate cost to you).	Premium SLA with guaranteed response times (high value to them, moderate cost to you).	Premium SLA with guaranteed response times (high value to them, moderate cost to you).
Fracture Zone Item (Held Constant Across Packages)	Shared marketing initiatives to enhance brand visibility for both parties.	Shared marketing initiatives to enhance brand visibility for both parties.	Shared marketing initiatives to enhance brand visibility for both parties.

Lead with Concessions

We discussed concessions earlier in the book, but as a reminder, these are the trade points you are willing to concede in a negotiation. During the planning and preparations phase, you want to be very strategic about listing and organizing your concessions, so there's no question about what triggers a concession and when in the negotiation process a trade point might come into play.

By leading with concession opportunities in your UNO Comparison Matrix, you demonstrate your flexibility and give the other side a sense of immediate victory. This sets the stage for a more collaborative negotiation by signaling goodwill. When the other side perceives they are making progress from the outset, they are more likely to engage positively and reciprocate with openness and cooperation. Strategically structuring your concessions allows you to control the negotiation flow, guiding discussions toward your priorities while maintaining leverage. It also fosters trust and momentum, reducing resistance when introducing your nonnegotiables or key deal points later in the conversation. However, it's essential that these initial concessions are low-cost to you but high-value to the other party—meaning they feel like they've won something significant without you sacrificing anything critical. This ensures you maintain strength in the negotiation while maximizing perceived value for both sides.

Create a Tiered Pricing Model

If you're negotiating the purchase of services or products, it will be important to justify your pricing. This is a critical step in any purchase negotiation. Reference comparable past transactions to demonstrate your rates are competitive and reflective of market standards. Consider introducing different pricing levels based on the scope of service or degree of involvement. You might even consider creating a Pricing-Tier Flowchart to take to the negotiations, making it easy for them to choose a tier that meets their needs.

- *Tier 1:* Basic service package with minimal features.
- *Tier 2:* Standard package with additional features and support.
- *Tier 3:* Premium package with comprehensive services and personalized support.

Decide Whether to Bundle or Unbundle

Sometimes it's advantageous to combine multiple benefits to enhance the appeal of your offer or solution. In these cases, present a variety of options along with their unique benefits. This approach not only provides flexibility but demonstrates your willingness to meet various needs and preferences. For example, when negotiating a software deal, including training sessions can add considerable value, making the entire package more enticing. By offering diverse and well-rounded proposals, you increase the likelihood of finding common ground and achieving a positive outcome.

On the flip side, sometimes it's advantageous to break down a complex offer or solution into simpler, more manageable parts to facilitate a smoother negotiation, especially in more intricate business deals. This approach helps clarify each component, making it easier for both parties to understand and discuss. Be ready to make strategic trade-offs, after planning them carefully, to maintain a strong negotiating position. However, it's equally important to ensure the other side does not cherry-pick their favorable elements from your proposals. That's why presenting each option as a cohesive unit is crucial. Any trade-offs you make should contribute to the overall integrity and value of the deal without making your UNO an à la carte menu. This method allows for clearer communication and more effective progress toward a successful agreement.

Prepare Compelling Incentives

There are a host of incentives you can prepare in advance and keep in your back pocket during a tough negotiation. Here's a list of some of the more popular perks:

- **Early Payment Perks:** When negotiating the sale of services or products, consider offering a significant discount or additional premium features when payment is made up front. You can create a discount calculator to determine the discount percentage based on payment terms (e.g., 5 percent discount for payment within ten days). You can do a break-even analysis to calculate the financial impact of offering this discount versus the benefits of improved cash flow. You can even create a client proposal template to outline the early payment terms, benefits, and conditions.

- **Volume-Based Benefits:** Leverage data to illustrate how increased purchase quantities can lead to significant financial gains for both parties. You can create a Volume Discount Matrix that defines the volume tiers (e.g., 10–20 units, 21–50 units, 51+ units) and assign discount rates to each tier. You can even analyze the financial impact in advance so you are ready to present the potential savings for the client based on their anticipated purchase volume.

- **Exclusivity Discounts:** If being the sole provider is crucial to the client, recommend a discounted rate in return for their commitment to avoid collaborations with competitors for a specified period. For efficient use of negotiating time, you can create an exclusivity contract template that includes a clause with the terms of exclusivity, including duration and scope as well as the discount structure that defines the discounts offered in exchange for exclusivity. Consider including a renewal option for the exclusivity agreement at the end of the term.

- **KPI-Driven Testimonials:** To sweeten up your negotiation, encourage the client to provide referrals or share their experience as a success story if specific key performance indicators (KPIs) are strong. You can create a KPI tracker that identifies KPIs that are critical to the client's success, as well as create a milestone chart that tracks progress toward these KPIs throughout the partnership. You can even create a testimonial-request template to ask for testimonials once KPIs are achieved, including suggested content and format.

- **Public Recognition Incentives:** Offer the client more favorable rates in exchange for their agreement to publicly identify as a user of your services. You can create a public endorsement agreement and plan in advance of the negotiation. It can clearly define the terms of this incentive as well as explain how you will leverage the client's endorsement across various channels (social media, case studies, press releases, etc.). Offer to provide an annual performance review to regularly assess the impact of the endorsement on brand credibility and new business opportunities.

- **Commit to On-Site Support:** For contractual services, you can propose that a specialized team to be present on-site for the initial quarter to ensure a seamless and impactful implementation. Create an on-site support plan that defines roles and responsibilities of the on-site support team. Develop an implementation timeline for the on-site period, including key milestones and deliverables. Create a system for gathering client feedback during the on-site period, allowing for real-time adjustments.

Prevent the Menu Effect

To prevent the other negotiating party from treating the UNO Comparison Matrix like a menu from which they can pick and choose, it's essential to establish clear rules from the outset. Clarify that each package is designed as a cohesive unit, where the elements work together to create value. Present the matrix in a way that emphasizes the trade-offs involved in each option, making it clear that selecting elements from different packages would disrupt the balance and reduce the overall effectiveness of the deal. Use visuals to highlight the interconnectedness and synergies of each package, reinforcing that the value is maximized only when the components are kept together.

It's important to begin with a broad overview to set the context and capture attention, then gradually narrow down to the specific details of each proposal in the matrix. Once you have covered the particulars, conclude with a broad summary that reinforces the key points and the overall vision. Throughout the presentation, highlight the comprehensive value of your offerings. Confidently communicate the possibilities that lie ahead while maintaining focus on the overall agreement. Highlight the long-term vision and the positive impact it can bring, ensuring everyone stays aligned with the bigger picture. This approach helps to inspire and motivate all parties, reinforcing the significance and potential of the deal.

If one proposal in the matrix isn't received favorably, you can seamlessly transition to another without losing momentum. This strategy keeps the negotiation dynamic and adaptable, demonstrating your preparedness and flexibility. Carefully plan your trade-offs within each package to ensure each alternative is compelling and aligned with your goals. This proactive approach allows you to maintain control of the negotiation process and increases your chances of finding a solution that meets everyone's needs.

UNOs Are Dynamic

Though you want to minimize the menu effect, you also want to approach each negotiation with flexibility and a willingness to modify your Unified Negotiation Options to account for new information or shifts in priorities. Recognize that negotiations are dynamic and evolving, and the ability to adapt is a testament to your strategic acumen and commitment to achieving the best possible outcomes. Embrace the process with humility, understanding that new insights and changing circumstances can provide valuable opportunities for growth and improvement. By being ready to update your UNO, you demonstrate a proactive and responsive mindset, showing your counterparts that you are genuinely invested in finding solutions that meet the evolving needs of all parties involved. This willingness to adjust your approach underscores your dedication to collaboration and mutual success. For instance, if new data emerges that impacts the feasibility of certain deal points, or if the other party's priorities shift during the course of discussions, being able to seamlessly incorporate these changes into your UNO ensures you remain aligned with the ultimate goals of the negotiation. This adaptability not only enhances your credibility and effectiveness but also fosters a positive and constructive negotiation atmosphere, where all parties feel heard and respected. Ultimately, your readiness to modify your UNO as needed positions you as a thoughtful, strategic, and empathetic negotiator who is committed to achieving excellence and creating lasting, beneficial partnerships.

Conclusion

Orchestrating a negotiation with a UNO Comparison Matrix allows you to package and present the right elements in the perfect sequence, creating a whole that is greater than the sum of its parts. By learning this packaging, you can seamlessly integrate all the key principles into a cohesive and compelling strategy. This skill elevates your negotiating position, ultimately setting the stage for successful outcomes with greater efficiency and effectiveness. The UNO Comparison Matrix is your key to structuring and delivering these comprehensive packages effectively. By ensuring your options are viewed as complete offerings, you maximize the strategic impact of your presentation and move toward outcomes that are balanced, mutually beneficial, and aligned with your overarching goals.

Notes

_____

_____

_____

_____

_____

_____

_____

_____

_____

_____

_____

_____

_____

_____

_____

_____

_____

_____

_____

_____

_____

_____

_____

_____

_____

_____

_____

_____

_____

**LIFE IS
NEGOTIATION.**

— Chris Voss

FINAL WRAP-UP

NO ONE CAN go through life—or even a single day—without negotiating *something*. As humans, it's what we do. And yet, very few people take the time to learn about negotiation. Here's to you for making the time to read *The Negotiation Code*. We've explored many topics and strategies in our journey through this book, and I hope you've found its contents useful.

Negotiation is part art, part science. By sharing my expertise and experience, hopefully I've helped you crack *The Negotiation Code*. It's why I wrote the book for you. As I've said several times in these pages, negotiation is a journey that never truly ends. But as long as you commit to growth, keep refining your approach, and lead with authenticity, you will not only succeed—you will thrive.

There are a few important ideas that I hope you will take away from this experience. First, it's important to remember that negotiation is much more than a set of skills; it's a mindset, a discipline, and a lifelong journey. In the twenty-first century, understanding how to effectively negotiate isn't an option; it's an essential leadership trait rooted in both ancient human instincts and modern strategic thinking. Second, a negotiation mindset can always be improved through training and discipline. Much like a muscle, your negotiation mindset needs to be exercised daily—or else it weakens. It's a use-it-or-lose-it situation. As long as you are willing to do the work, you'll improve. It takes practice, but I promise it's worth the effort.

We have seen how artificial intelligence, once a distant concept, is now playing an active role in shaping the way we approach negotiation and decision-making. While AI can enhance strategy and provide insights, hopefully this book has helped you to understand that the true art of negotiation remains deeply human—anchored in emotional intelligence, social awareness, adaptability, and an unwavering commitment to personal and professional growth. Those who master *The Negotiation Code* understand that it takes both AI tools and human EQ, SQ, and AQ to get the job done in *any* negotiation—be it professional or personal. This, paired with the ten strategies presented in this book, serve as a powerful road map toward success and sustainable outcomes. Together, they will guide you from preparation to execution, ensuring that every negotiation in which you are involved leads to meaningful outcomes.

At its core, negotiation is about bringing your best self and tools to the table and creating value. It's about fostering relationships built on trust, mutual respect, and shared success. The most effective negotiators understand that preparation, clarity of purpose, and the ability to listen and adapt are just as critical as the tactics and strategies employed at the bargaining table. The three pillars—strategic planning, multiple intelligences, and continuous growth—are the foundation upon which all successful negotiations are built. They lead to alignment, which in turn leads to optimal outcomes and sustainable results.

Whether you are securing a business deal, advocating for yourself in the workplace, or navigating a complex personal decision, applying the strategies explored in *The Negotiation Code* will empower you to approach every situation with confidence, intelligence, and integrity.

The future belongs to those who can navigate complexity, adapt to change, and communicate effectively. By embracing *The Negotiation Code*, you are positioning yourself as a leader who can drive innovation, build strong partnerships, and create lasting impact. It's time to put the insights in *The Negotiation Code* into action. Go forth and negotiate with confidence. I'd love to hear from readers, so let me know how it goes.

NEGOTIATION DOS AND DON'TS RECAP

Negotiation Dos

Seize the Opportunity: Embrace every chance to ask for what you need or want. Remember, opportunities often arise from simply making the request. By confidently seizing the moment, you open the door to possibilities that might otherwise remain unexplored. Taking initiative and expressing your needs assertively can lead to unexpected and positive outcomes.

Assess the Need for a Discussion: Carefully evaluate whether negotiation is the most appropriate course of action for your specific situation. Not every scenario requires negotiation, so it's important to consider if this approach will best serve your goals. By thoughtfully assessing the need for a discussion, you ensure you are entering negotiations with purpose and clarity.

Equip Yourself for Success: Equip yourself with the knowledge, strategies, and techniques to enhance your readiness and confidence. Preparation is key to navigating negotiations effectively and achieving your desired outcomes. You can use this book as your essential tool kit to prepare thoroughly for any impending negotiations

Understand Your Biases: Recognize and acknowledge your own biases, as these can significantly influence your negotiation approach. Learn strategies to avoid being anchored by preconceived notions or habitual thinking patterns. By understanding and managing your biases, you can approach negotiations with greater objectivity and fairness.

Set Clear Objectives: Define your goals clearly before entering into negotiations to guide your efforts effectively. Knowing what you want to achieve provides direction and focus, helping you to stay on track throughout the negotiation process. Clear objectives also allow you to measure success and make informed decisions.

Build Rapport: Establish a genuine connection with the other party to enhance communication and understanding. Building rapport creates a positive atmosphere and fosters a sense of mutual respect. By taking the time to connect on a personal level, you can lay the foundation for more productive and meaningful negotiations.

Listen Actively: Show genuine interest in the other party's perspective and needs to foster a productive dialogue. Active listening involves fully engaging with what the other person is saying, asking clarifying questions, and demonstrating empathy. This approach helps to build a deeper understanding and creates an environment in which both parties feel heard and valued.

Distinguish Individuals from Their Concerns: Understand that emotions and viewpoints can differ from the main issues at hand. By separating these elements, you can nurture more effective and constructive relationships. Acknowledging the human element in negotiations allows you to address concerns without letting emotions derail the process.

Explore New Ideas: Encourage the generation of creative ideas and embrace originality to find solutions that resonate with everyone involved. Foster a culture of innovation in your discussions and remain open to unconventional approaches. By exploring new ideas, you can discover pathways to agreement that may not have been initially apparent.

Counter Fixed Stances: If the other party is inflexible, redirect the conversation to the underlying principles of the deal. Focus on the core values and objectives that are driving the negotiation and seek common ground. This approach helps break down rigid positions and facilitates more productive discussions.

Remain Vigilant to Unfair Tactics: Identify and address unfair tactics courteously, steering the discussion back to constructive negotiation principles. Be aware of manipulative behaviors and respond with integrity, ensuring the negotiation remains fair and respectful. By maintaining your composure and commitment to ethical practices, you can uphold the integrity of the process.

Unify Aims: Identify shared goals and steer discussions toward achieving them, creating a common purpose. Highlight the areas where your interests align with those of the other party and work together to pursue these shared objectives. By focusing on common aims, you can build a sense of unity and drive the negotiation toward a successful conclusion.

Embrace Diverse Possibilities: Stay flexible and open to unexpected solutions, adapting as necessary to reach an agreement. Recognize that the best outcomes often come from being willing to entertain a range of possibilities. By embracing diverse options, you can navigate the negotiation process with agility and creativity, ultimately finding solutions that satisfy all parties involved.

Be Transparent to Build Trust: Foster an environment of openness by sharing relevant information, intentions, and constraints honestly. Transparency builds credibility and removes doubts, paving the way for deeper trust and collaboration. By clearly communicating your priorities and acknowledging challenges, you create a foundation for mutual understanding. Trust thrives when both parties feel secure in the authenticity of the exchange, allowing negotiations to progress with confidence and clarity.

Negotiation Don'ts

Issue Ultimatums: Avoid using inflammatory phrases like "Take it or leave it," or "This is my final offer." Such statements can create unnecessary tension and close off avenues for dialogue. Instead, focus on keeping the conversation open and constructive, exploring options that can lead to a mutually satisfying agreement.

Apply Excessive Pressure: Don't strong-arm the other party into submission. High-pressure tactics can damage relationships and lead to resentment. Aim for a respectful and balanced approach that encourages cooperation and understanding, fostering a more positive negotiation atmosphere.

Exploit Power Dynamics: Refrain from abusing a position of power or taking advantage of the upper hand. Leveraging power unethically can erode trust and hinder long-term relationships. Approach negotiations with a sense of fairness and equity, ensuring both parties feel valued and respected.

Neglect the Relationship: Remember, a successful negotiation is not just a onetime transaction but a foundation for long-term partnerships. Focus on building and maintaining positive relationships, which can lead to future opportunities and collaborative success.

Assume a Zero-Sum Outcome: Don't treat the negotiation as if one party's gain is the other's loss. Aim for outcomes that benefit both parties, recognizing that creating value for everyone involved can lead to more sustainable and rewarding agreements.

Say Dismissive Statements: Refrain from saying things like "That's not my problem," or "You're being unreasonable." Such statements can make the other party feel dismissed. Instead, strive for language that keeps the conversation open and respectful.

Promote Constructive Dialogue: Avoid phrases like "Why would I ever agree to that?" or "I've given you everything you've asked for." These can come across as defensive or accusatory. Focus on understanding the other party's perspective and finding common ground.

Ignore Empathy: Never say, "I don't care about your concerns," or "That's the best we can do." Such statements can shut down dialogue and alienate the other party. Show empathy and a willingness to consider their needs and concerns.

Close Discussions: Avoid saying, "That's not up for discussion," or "We've always done it this way." These phrases can stifle innovation and flexibility. Be open to exploring new ideas and approaches that can lead to better outcomes.

Be Negative: Refrain from using outright negatives like "No," or "That's your responsibility, not mine." Negative statements can hinder progress. Instead, frame your responses in a positive and constructive manner.

Ignore Time and Effort: Avoid saying, "You're wasting my time," or "If you don't like it, find someone else." Such statements can damage the negotiation process and relationships. Show respect for the time and effort of all parties involved.

Let Go of Professionalism: Never end a conversation abruptly with phrases like "This conversation is over," or "I don't need to explain myself." Maintain professionalism by keeping the lines of communication open and transparent.

Forget Flexibility: Avoid saying, "It's nonnegotiable," or "Don't take it personally." These statements can create barriers. Encourage flexibility and understanding in the negotiation process.

Limit Understanding: Avoid statements like "That's just how it is," or "If you were in my position, you'd understand." Strive to foster understanding and empathy, recognizing the perspectives and positions of the other party.

By avoiding these negative statements and approaches, you can create a more positive, respectful, and effective negotiation environment that encourages cooperation and successful outcomes.

ACKNOWLEDGMENTS

First and foremost, I want to thank my family—my true foundation.

Alexa, you are my guiding star, my constant source of strength and love. Our girls, Allie and Leah, remind me daily that the most meaningful negotiations happen at home, where love, patience, and understanding are at the center of everything.

To my mom, my first mentor, thank you for showing me that anything is possible and for always being my North Star. To my late dad, I strive every day to live up to your incredible drive for excellence, knowing you're watching over me with pride.

Jade, my sister, and Joel, my brother-in-law—you've been unwavering in your support, friendship, and belief in me.

Uncle Shaun, thank you for giving me that push when I needed it most and for teaching me to think big. Your guidance has been a game-changer at crucial moments in my life.

To my grandparents Rene and Archie, your love and lessons during my formative years shaped the person I am today.

To the team that stood by me through challenges and triumphs:

Craig, Ilan, Gavin, Karen, and my core support circle—your care, encouragement, and belief in me during tough times meant the world. You've been more than a support system; you've been my lifeline.

To my professors, teachers, and the incredible network I've built at Kellogg, thank you for giving me the tools and inspiration to pair learning with experience. Your contributions have been vital to my growth.

To my YPO family, thank you for challenging me to lead with greater purpose and for enriching my perspective on life and leadership.

To my professional partners and collaborators:

Thank you for your trust and shared vision. You've made the journey as meaningful as it is rewarding.

To everyone who's ever sought my advice, placed faith in me, or supported me during tough times, know this: your trust inspires me to work harder, dream bigger, and push through every obstacle.

To my friends—my chosen family:

You've been my joy and my strength, proving the best successes in life are the ones we share.

A heartfelt thank-you to everyone who helped bring this book to life:

From the early feedback to the editing and publishing, your collective efforts turned an idea into something real and impactful.

Finally, to you, the reader, thank you for investing your time in this book. I hope it empowers you to unlock the art of negotiation and transform your life and career.

Here's to your success,
Guy

BIBLIOGRAPHY

Ames, Daniel R., and Malia F. Mason. "Tandem Anchoring: Informational and Politeness Effects of Range Offers in Social Exchange." *Journal of Personality and Social Psychology* 108, no. 2 (2015): 254–274.

Babcock, Linda, and George Loewenstein. "Explaining Bargaining Impasse: The Role of Self-Serving Biases." *Journal of Economic Perspectives* 11, no. 1(1997): 109–126.

Babcock, Linda, and Sara Laschever. *Women Don't Ask: The High Cost of Avoiding Negotiation—and Positive Strategies for Change.* New York: Bantam, 2007.

Babcock, Linda, and Sara Laschever. *Women Don't Ask: Negotiation and the Gender Divide.* Princeton, NJ: Princeton University Press, 2003.

Baltes, Boris, Marcus Dickson, Michael Sherman, and Cara Bauer. "Computer-Mediated Communication and Group Decision Making: A Meta-Analysis." *Organizational Behavior and Human Decision Processes* 87, no. 1 (2002): 156–179.

Bercovitch, J., and R. Jackson. "Conflict Resolution in the Twenty-first Century: Principles, Methods, and Approaches." *Journal of Conflict Resolution* 53, no. 1 (2003), 3–41.

Brehm, Jack W. "Postdecision Changes in the Desirability of Alternatives." *The Journal of Abnormal and Social Psychology* 52, no. 3 (1956): 384.

Brown, Nicola, Daniel Read, and Barbara Summers. "The Lure of Choice." *Journal of Behavioral Decision Making* 16, no. 4 (2003): 297–308.

Bunkley, Nick. "With Low Prices, Hyundai Builds Market Share." *The New York Times*, September 21, 2009, https://www.nytimes.com/2009/09/22/business/global/22hyundai.html.

Carnegie, Dale. *How to Win Friends and Influence People.* New York: Simon and Schuster, 1936.

Carnevale, P. J., and D. H. Choi. "Culture in the Mediation of International Disputes." *International Negotiation* 5, no. 2 (2000), 319–344.

Carnevale, Peter, Kathleen O'Connor, and Christopher McCusker. "Time Pressure in Negotiation and Mediation." In *Time Pressure and Stress in Human Judgment and Decision Making.* New York: Springer, 1993.

Chou, E. Y., and J. K. Murnighan. "Life or Death Decisions: Framing the Call for Help." PLoS ONE 8, no.3 (2013). https://doi.org/10.1371/journal.pone.0057351.

Cialdini, R. B. *Influence: The Psychology of Persuasion.* Harper #dBusiness, (2006).

Colvin, Geoff. "The Hidden—But Very Real—Cost of Working from Home." *Fortune*, August 10, 2020. https://fortune.com/2020/08/10/remote-work-from-home-cost-zoom-innovation-google-goldman-sachs/.

de Luca, Federico, and Andrew Hinde. (2016). "Effectiveness of the 'Back-to-Sleep' Campaigns Among Healthcare Professionals in the Past 20 Years: A Systematic Review."

BMJ Open 6, no. 9 (2016). https://bmjopen.bmj.com/content/6/9/e011435.

De Martino, Benedetto, Dharshan Kumaran, Ben Seymour, and Raymond J. Dolan. "Frames, Biases, and Rational Decision-Making in the Human Brain." *Science* 313(5787) (2006): 684-7. https://www.science.org/doi/10.1126/science.1128356.

Druckman, D., & Olekalns, M. (2013). Punctuated negotiations: transitions, interruptions, and turning points. https://researchers.mq.edu.au/en/publications/punctuated-negotiations-transitions-interruptions-and-turning-poi?utm_source=chatgpt.com

Epley, Nicholas, and Thomas Gilovich. "When Effortful Thinking Influences Judgmental Anchoring: Differential Effects of Forewarning and Incentives on Self-Generated and Externally Provided Anchors." *Journal of Behavioral Decision-Making* 18, no.3 (2005): 199-212. https://doi.org/10.1002/bdm.495.

Fearon, J. D. "Why Do Some Civil Wars Last So Much Longer than Others?" *Journal of Conflict Resolution* 48, no.2 (2004): 275-301. https://doi.org/10.1177/0022343304043770

Fisher, Roger, William Ury, and Bruce Patton. *Getting to Yes: Negotiating Agreement Without Giving In*. Penguin Books, 2011.

Franconeri, Steven, Andrew Hollingworth, and Daniel J. Simons. "Do New Objects Capture Attention?" *Psychological Science* 16, no.4 (2005): 275–281. https://doi.org/10.1111/j.0956-7976.2005.01528.x

Freedman, Jonathan L., and Scott C. Fraser. "Compliance Without Pressure: The Foot-in-the-Door Technique." *Journal of Personality and Social Psychology* 4, no.2 (1966): 195–202. http://dx.doi.org/10.1037/h0023552.

Galinsky, Adam D., and Thomas Mussweiler. "First Offers as Anchors: The Role of Perspective-Taking and Negotiator Focus." *Journal of Personality and Social Psychology* 81, no.4 (2001): 657–669. https://doi.org/10.1037/0022-3514.81.4.657

Galinsky, Adam D., Gillian Ku, and Thomas Mussweiler. "To Start Low or to Start High? The Case of Auctions Versus Negotiations." *Current Directions in Psychological Science* 18, no.6 (2009): 357–361. https://doi.org/10.1111/j.1467-8721.2009.01667.x

Galinsky, Adam D., Thomas Mussweiler, and Victoria Medvec. "Disconnecting Outcomes and Evaluations: The Role of Negotiator Focus." *Journal of Personality and Social Psychology* 83, no.5 (2002): 1131–1140. http://dx.doi.org/10.1037//0022-3514.83.5.1131

Galinsky, Adam D., Vanessa Seiden, Peter Kim, and Victoria Medvec. "The Dissatisfaction of Having Your First Offer Accepted: The Role of Counterfactual Thinking in Negotiations." *Personality and Social Psychology Bulletin* 28, no.2 (2002): 271–283. https://doi.org/10.1177/0146167202282012

Gallo, Amy. "Setting the Record Straight: Using an Outside Offer to Get a Raise." *Harvard Business Review*, July 5, 2016. https://hbr.org/2016/07/setting-the-record-straight-using-an-outside-offer-to-get-a-raise.

Gilbert, Daniel T., and Jane E. J. Ebert. "Decisions and Revisions: The Affective Forecasting of Changeable Outcomes." *Journal of Personality and Social Psychology* 82, no.4 (2002): 503–514. https://doi.org/10.1037/0022-3514.82.4.503.

Harnett, Donald and Larry Cummings. *Bargaining Behavior: An International Study*. Dane Publications, 1980.

Heneman, Herbert G. "Comparisons of Self- and Superior Ratings of Managerial Performance." *Journal of Applied Psychology* 59, no.5 (1974): 638-642. http://dx.doi.org/10.1037/h0037341.

Hughes, Jonathan, Jeff Weiss, Stuart Kliman, and David Chapnick. "Negotiation Systems and Strategies." In International Contract Manual. Thomson Reuters, 2019.

Hughes, Jonathan, and Danny Ertel. "What's Your Negotiation Strategy?" *Harvard Business Review*, July 2020. https://hbr.org/2020/07/whats-your-negotiation-strategy.

Job, R., and F. Soames. "Effective and Ineffective Use of Fear in Health Promotion Campaigns." *American Journal of Public Health* 78, no.2 (1988). https://doi.org/10.2105/AJPH.78.2.163

Jones, Edward E., and Richard. E. Nisbett. "The Actor and the Observer: Divergent Perceptions of the Causes of Behavior. In E. E. Jones, D. E. Kanouse, H. H. Kelley, R. E. Nisbett, S. Valins, and B. Weiner (Eds.), Attribution: Perceiving the Causes of Behavior (pp. 79–94)." Mahway, NJ: Lawrence Erlbaum.

Jönsson, C. "Diplomacy, Bargaining and Negotiation." In *Handbook of International Relations*. http://doi.org/10.4135/9781848608290.n11

Kahneman, D. *Thinking, Fast and Slow*. Farrar, Straus, and Giroux, 2011.

Kahneman, Daniel, and Amos Tversky. "Prospect Theory: An Analysis of Decision Under Risk." *Econometrica* 47, no.2 (1979): 263-292. https://doi.org/10.2307/1914185.

Kahneman, Daniel, Jack Knetsch, and Richard Thaler. "Anomalies: The Endowment Effect, Loss Aversion, and Status Quo Bias." *Journal of Economic Perspectives* 5, no.1 (1991): 193–206. https://www.jstor.org/stable/1942711.

Kahneman, Daniel, Jack Knetsch, and Richard Thaler. "Experimental Tests of the Endowment Effect and the Coase Theorem." *Journal of Political Economy* 98, no.6 (1990): 1325–1348. http://dx.doi.org/10.1086/261737.

Karrass, C. L. *Give and Take: The Complete Guide to Negotiating Strategies and Tactics.* Thomas Y. Crowell Co, 1974.

Karrass, Chester L. *The Negotiating Game: How to Get What You Want.* Harper Business, 1992.

Kerr, Steven. *Reward Systems: Does Yours Measure Up?* Harvard Business School Press, 2008.

Kiesler, S., and L. Sproull. "Group Decision Making and Communication Technology." *Organizational Behavior and Human Decision Processes* 52, no.1 (1992): 96–123. https://doi.org/10.1016/0749-5978(92)90047-B.

Kolb, D. M., and Putnam, L. L. "The Multiple Faces of Conflict and Negotiation in Organizations." *Negotiation Journal* 8 no.3 (1992): 215-234. https://www.jstor.org/stable/i342662

Kotter, J. P. (2013). "Three Keys to Influencing Others." Harvard Business Review, accessed June 20, 2025. https://hbr.org/video/2363621373001/three-keys-to-influencing-others.

Leonardelli, Geoffrey, Jun Gu, Geordie McRuer, Victoria Medvec, and Adam D. Galinsky. "Multiple Equivalent Simultaneous Offers (MESOs) Reduce the Negotiator Dilemma: How a Choice of First Offers Increases Economic and Relational Outcomes." *Organizational Behavior and Human Decision Processes* 152 (2019): 64–83. https://doi.org/10.1016/j.obhdp.2019.01.007.

Leshner, Glenn, Paul Bolls, and Kevin Wise. "Motivated Processing of Fear Appeal and Disgust Images in Televised Anti-Tobacco Ads." *Journal of Media*

Psychology: Theories, Methods, and Applications 23, no.2 (2011): 77–89. http://dx.doi.org/10.1027/1864-1105/a000037.

Lewicki, Roy J., Bruce Barry, and David M. Saunders. "Zone of Potential Agreement." In *Negotiation* (7th ed.). McGraw-Hill Education, 2015.

Lytle, Anne L., Jeanne Brett, and Debra Shapiro. "The Strategic Use of Interests, Rights, and Power to Resolve Disputes." *Negotiation Journal* 15, no.1 (1999): 31–52. https://doi.org/10.1111/j.1571-9979.1999.tb00178.x.

Magee, Joe C., Adam D. Galinsky, and Deborah H. Gruenfeld. "Power, Propensity to Negotiate, and Moving First in Competitive Interactions." *Personality and Social Psychology Bulletin* 33, no.2 (2007): 200–212. https://doi.org/10.1177/0146167206294413.

Malhotra, D., and Bazerman, M. H. *Negotiation Genius: How to Overcome Obstacles and Achieve Brilliant Results at the Bargaining Table and Beyond.* Bantam, 2007.

Malito, Alessandra. "More Americans Are Leaving Their Money in 401(k) Plans After Retirement—Should You?" *MarketWatch*, Oct. 31, 2019. https://www.marketwatch.com/story/more-americans-are-leaving-their-money-in-401k-plans-after-retirement-should-you-2019-10-31

Medvec, V. *Negotiate Without Fear.* Wiley, 2021.

Menkel-Meadow, C. "Toward Another View of Legal Negotiation: The Structure of Problem Solving." *Negotiation Journal* 20, no.2 (2004): 151-179. https://doi.org/10.1093/oso/9780197513248.003.0011

Miller, George A. "The Magical Number Seven, Plus or Minus Two: Some Limits on Our Capacity for Processing Information." *Psychological Review* 63 (1956): 81–97. https://doi.org/10.1037/h0043158

Moore, C. W. *The Mediation Process: Practical Strategies for Resolving Conflict.* Jossey-Bass, 2014.

Narayanan, Jayanth, Ivy Buche, Lindsay McTeague, Amit Joshi, and Maude Lavanchy. "The Art and Science of Negotiation." *International Institute for Management Development*, February 2018. https://www.imd.org/research-knowledge/articles/negotiation-skills-to-achieve-positive-outcomes/.

Advancing AI Negotiations: New Theory and Evidence from a Large-Scale Autonomous Negotiations Competition

Michelle Vaccaro, Michael Caoson, Harang Ju, Sinan Aral, and Jared R. Curhan*

*Corresponding author: curhan@mit.edu

Newcomb, Theodore M. "Varieties of Interpersonal Attraction." In *Group Dynamics: Research and Theory,* edited by D. Cartwright and A. Zander. Row, Peterson, 1960.

Brian Ibbotson Groth, Sølvi Glevoll; A New Use for Practitioners in Teaching Negotiation. Negotiation Journal 2007; 23 (2): 173–184. doi: https://doi.org/10.1111/j.1571-9979.2007.00135.x

Peppet, S. "Unraveling Privacy: Data Brokerage, Privacy, and the Tools of Influence." *Harvard Journal on Legislation* 38 (2010): 317.

Pruitt, Dean G. "Negotiation Behavior." Academic Press, 1981.

Purdy, Jill Pete Nye, and P. V. (Sundar) Balakrishnan. "The Impact of Communication Media on Negotiation Outcomes." *International Journal of Conflict Management* 11, no.2 (2000): 162–187. https://doi.org/10.1108/eb022839.

Raiffa, Howard. *The Art and Science of Negotiation.* Belknap Press, 1982.

Ross, Michael, and Fiore Sicoly. "Egocentric Biases in Availability and Attribution." *Journal of Personality and Social Psychology* 37, no.3 (1979): 322–336. https://doi.org/10.1037/0022-3514.37.3.322.

Schraer, Michael, Mary Kern, Gail Berger, and Victoria Medvec. "The Illusion of Transparency in Performance Appraisals: When and Why Accuracy Motivation Explains Unintentional Feedback Inflation." *Organizational Behavior and Human Decision Processes* 144 (2018): 171–186.

Schweinsberg, Martin, Gillian Ku, Cynthia S. Wang, and Madan M. Pilluta. "Starting High and Ending with Nothing: The Role of Anchors and Power in Negotiations." *Journal of Experimental Social Psychology* 48, no.1 (2012): 226–231.

Shell, G. R. *Bargaining for Advantage: Negotiation Strategies for Reasonable People.* Penguin Books, 2006.

Sinaceur, Marwan, William Maddux, Dmitri Vasiljevic, Ricardo Perez Nuquel, and Adam D. Galinsky. "Good Things Come to Those Who Wait: Late First Offers Facilitate Creative Agreements in Negotiation." *Personality and Social Psychology Bulletin* 39 no.6 (2013): 814–825. https://doi.org/10.1177/0146167213483319.

Straus, Susan G., and Joseph E. McGrath. "Does the Medium Matter? The Interaction of Task Type and Technology on Group Performance and Member Reactions." *Journal of Applied Psychology* 79, no.1 (1994): 87–97. https://doi.org/10.1037/0021-9010.79.1.87.

Swaab, Roderick, and Adam D. Galinsky. "How to Negotiate When You're (Literally) Far Apart." *Negotiation* 10, no.2 (2007): 7–9.

Swaab, Roderick, Mary Kern, Daniel Diermeier, and Victoria Medvec. "Who Says What to Whom? The Impact of Communication Setting and Channel on Exclusion from Multiparty Negotiation Agreements." *Social Cognition* 27 no.3 (2009): 385–401. https://doi.org/10.1521/soco.2009.27.3.385.

Theeuwes, J., A. F. Kramer, S. Hahn, and D. E. Irwin. "Our Eyes Do Not Always Go Where We Want Them to Go: Capture of the Eyes by New Objects." *Psychological Science* 9, no.5 (1998): 379–385. https://doi.org/10.1111/1467-9280.00071.

Thompson, L. L. *The Mind and Heart of the Negotiator.* Pearson, 2014.

Thorndyke, Perry. W. "Cognitive Structures in Comprehension and Memory of Narrative Discourse." *Cognitive Psychology* 9 no.1 1977: 77–110. https://doi.org/10.1016/0010-0285(77)90005-6.

Tsaousides, Theo. "7 Things You Need to Know About Fear." *Smashing the Brainblocks* (blog), *Psychology Today*, November 19, 2015. https://www.psychologytoday.com/us/blog/smashing-the-brainblocks/201511/7-things-you-need-know-about-fear.

Tversky, Amos, and Daniel Kahneman. "Availability: A Heuristic for Judging Frequency and Probability." *Cognitive Psychology* 5 (1973): 207–232. https://doi.org/10.1016/0010-0285(73)90033-9.

Tversky, Amos, and Daniel Kahneman. "Judgment Under Uncertainty: Heuristics and Biases." *Science* 185, no.4157 (1974): 1124–1131. https://doi.org/10.1126/science.185.4157.1124.

Tversky, Amos, and Daniel Kahneman. "The Framing of Decisions and the Psychology of Choice." *Science* 211, no.4481 (1981): 453–458. https://doi.org/10.1126/science.7455683.

Ury, W. *Getting Past No: Negotiating in Difficult Situations.* Bantam, 1993.

Ury, William L., Jeanne Brett, and Stephen Goldberg. *Getting Disputes Resolved: Designing Systems to Cut the Costs of Conflict.* Jossey-Bass, 1988.

Valdes-Dapena, Peter. "Laid off? Hyundai Will Take Your Car Back." *CNN*, January 5, 2009. https://money.cnn.com/2009/01/05/autos/hyundai_assurance/index.htm.

Voss, C., and Raz, T. *Never Split the Difference: Negotiating As If Your Life Depended On It.* Harper Business, 2016.

Walter, B. F. "Why Bad Governance Leads to Repeat Civil War." *Journal of Conflict Resolution* 59 no.7 (2015): 1242-1272. https://doi.org/10.1177/0022002714528006.

Weiss, J., Donigian, A., and Hughes, J. "Extreme Negotiations." Harvard Business School Publishing Corporation, 2010.

Whyte, Glen, and James K. Sebenius. "The Effect of Multiple Anchors on Anchoring in Individual and Group Judgment." *Organizational Behavior and Human Decision Processes* 69 no.1 (1997): 74–85. https://doi.org/10.1006/obhd.1996.2674.

Zartman, I. W., and Rubin, J. Z. "The Study of Power and the Practice of Negotiation." *International Negotiation* 5 no.3 (2000): 341-356.

GLOSSARY

A

- **Active Listening** – Engaging fully in a conversation, demonstrating comprehension, and responding thoughtfully.
- **Adaptability Quotient (AQ)** – The ability to adjust to changing circumstances and respond effectively.
- **AI in Negotiation** – The use of artificial intelligence–driven tools to analyze data, predict outcomes, and optimize negotiation strategies.
- **Anchoring** – The practice of setting an initial reference point in a negotiation that influences the final outcome.
- **Artificial Intelligence (AI)** – Technology that can enhance negotiation by providing data analysis, predictions, and strategic recommendations.

B

- **Best Secondary Option (BSO™)** – A unique alternative to a negotiated agreement that maximizes leverage.
- **Body Language** – Nonverbal communication cues, such as posture, facial expressions, and gestures, that influence negotiations.

C

- **Case Studies** – Real-world examples used to illustrate negotiation strategies and outcomes.
- **Compelling Incentives** – Strategic perks used to persuade the other party during negotiations, such as volume discounts or exclusivity agreements.
- **Concessions** – Strategic trade-offs made during negotiation to reach a mutually beneficial agreement.
- **Customer Reliance** – A strategy to increase a client's dependency on your services by consistently delivering exceptional value.

D

- **Data-Driven Decision-Making** – Using analytics to guide negotiation strategies and decisions.
- **Define Purpose, Objectives, and Goals** – The process of clarifying what you aim to achieve in a negotiation.

E

- **Empathy Map** – A tool that analyzes the emotions, thoughts, and behaviors of negotiation counterparts.
- **Emotional Intelligence (EQ)** – The ability to recognize, understand, and manage emotions in oneself and others.
- **Endorsements** – Third-party validations, such as awards or client testimonials, that support negotiation claims.
- **Extended Engagement Strategy** – A method of fostering long-term collaboration rather than focusing solely on a single deal.

GLOSSARY

- **Exclusivity Discounts** – Offering reduced pricing in exchange for a commitment to avoid collaborations with competitors.

F

- **Facial Expressions** – Microexpressions and other facial cues that provide insights into a negotiator's emotions.
- **Fight-or-Flight Response** – The body's instinctive reaction to stress, which can impact negotiation performance.
- **Framing** – The way an offer or negotiation is positioned to influence perception and decision-making.

G

- **Gain Points** – Elements in a negotiation that add value for one or both parties.

I

- **Influence Strategy** – Methods used to shape perceptions and decisions in negotiation.
- **Intelligence Types in Negotiation**
- **Emotional Intelligence (EQ)** – Managing emotions for better negotiation outcomes.
- **Social Intelligence (SQ)** – Navigating social environments and relationships.
- **Adaptability Quotient (AQ)** – Responding effectively to change.

K

- **KPI-Driven Testimonials** –Referrals or success stories based on key performance indicators achieved.

L

- **Large Language Models (LLMs)** – AI-based systems that process and generate humanlike text, often used for negotiation support.
- **Loss Aversion Strategy** – A negotiation approach that leverages the human tendency to avoid losses rather than seek gains.

M

- **Managing Fight-or-Flight Responses** – Techniques for staying calm and composed in high-pressure negotiations.
- **Mirroring** – The subconscious or deliberate replication of another person's behavior or gestures to build rapport.
- **Motivate and Celebrate** – Recognizing and celebrating negotiation progress to boost morale and engagement.
- **Mutual Respect and Trust** – The foundation of effective negotiations and long-term business relationships.

N

- **Negotiating Grid™** – A structured framework for evaluating trade-offs, value creation, and potential concessions.

- **Negotiation Mindset** – The perspective that negotiation is a collaborative and strategic process rather than a win-or-lose scenario.

O

- **On-Site Support** – Offering in-person support to ensure smooth implementation of agreements.

P

- **People Skills** – The interpersonal abilities required to build trust, rapport, and influence in negotiations.
- **Planning and Preparation** – The dual process of mapping negotiation strategies and gathering necessary information.
- **Posture and Positioning** – Physical stance and orientation that convey confidence and engagement.
- **Proxemics** – The use of space in communication and negotiation to establish dominance, trust, or engagement.
- **Public Recognition Incentives** – A negotiation tactic where clients or partners are offered better terms in exchange for public endorsements.

R

- **Relationship Capital** – The value of trust and goodwill built over time in business interactions.
- **Role-Playing for Negotiation Training** – Practicing scenarios to enhance real-world negotiation skills.

S

- **Shared Success Outcome** – A negotiated agreement that benefits all parties involved.
- **Social Intelligence (SQ)** – The ability to navigate complex social environments and build meaningful relationships.
- **Steeple Gesture** – A hand position that conveys confidence and authority.
- **Strategic Alliances** – Long-term partnerships that create mutual benefits beyond a single negotiation.
- **Strategic Planning and Thinking** – The process of setting negotiation objectives and analyzing potential outcomes.
- **SWOT Analysis** – A method for evaluating strengths, weaknesses, opportunities, and threats in a negotiation.

T

- **Tiered Pricing Model** – A pricing structure that offers different levels of service or benefits.
- **Trade Points** – Negotiable aspects of a deal that can be used strategically.
- **Transparency in Negotiation** – The practice of being open and honest while maintaining strategic leverage.
- **Trust Building Techniques** – Methods such as honesty, vulnerability, and consistency that foster long-term trust in negotiations.

U

- **Ultimate Goals** – Long-term objectives that guide negotiation decisions beyond immediate outcomes.
- **Unique Selling Proposition (USP)** – The distinguishing value that sets an offer apart from competitors.

- **Unified Negotiation Options (UNO™)** – A strategic approach to presenting multiple offers in negotiations to maximize value and flexibility.
- **Uncomfortable Transparency** – The practice of being open and honest in negotiations, even when it is difficult.

V

- **Value Proposition** – A clear articulation of what makes an offer unique and compelling.
- **Volume-Based Benefits** – Discount structures that incentivize higher purchase quantities.

www.ingramcontent.com/pod-product-compliance
Lightning Source LLC
Chambersburg PA
CBHW071552210326
41597CB00019B/3215